W9-CZX-081

Publius

The Accessible
Federalist

Publius

The Accessible
Federalist

*A Modern English Translation of
16 Key Federalist Papers*

Adapted, with Introduction, by
S. Adam Seagrave

Hackett Publishing Company, Inc.
Indianapolis/Cambridge

Copyright © 2017 by Hackett Publishing Company, Inc.

All rights reserved
Printed in the United States of America

20 19 18 17   1 2 3 4 5 6 7

For further information, please address
Hackett Publishing Company, Inc.
P.O. Box 44937
Indianapolis, Indiana 46244-0937

www.hackettpublishing.com

Cover design by Brian Rak
Composition by Aptara, Inc.

Library of Congress Cataloging-in-Publication Data
Names: Seagrave, S. Adam, adapter.
Title: The accessible Federalist : a modern English translation of 16 key
    Federalist papers adapted, with introduction / by S. Adam Seagrave.
Description: Indianapolis ; Cambridge : Hackett Publishing Company, Inc.,
    [2017] | Includes index.
Identifiers: LCCN 2016035418 | ISBN 9781624665509 (pbk.) | ISBN
    9781624665516 (cloth)
Subjects: LCSH: Constitutional history—United States—Sources.
Classification: LCC KF4515 .F4 2017 | DDC 342.7302/9—dc23
LC record available at https://lccn.loc.gov/2016035418

The paper used in this publication meets the minimum requirements of
American National Standard for Information Sciences—Permanence of
Paper for Printed Library Materials, ANSI Z39.48–1984.

∞

Contents

Acknowledgments   *vii*

I.   Introduction   ix

II.   A Note on the Text   xvi

III. *The Federalist* Papers   1

No. 1—Introducing the Argument for
  the Constitution   1

No. 10—Solution to the Problems of Faction   4

No. 14—Pure Democracy versus Republic   9

No. 15—Problems with the Articles of
  Confederation   13

No. 37—The Constitution-Making Experience   18

No. 39—Republicanism and Federalism   24

No. 47—Separation of Powers   29

No. 49—Response to Jefferson's Democratic Ideas   35

No. 51—Ambition Counteracting Ambition   38

No. 54—Slavery and Representation:
  The Three-fifths Clause   42

No. 57—The House of Representatives   46

No. 62—The Senate   51

No. 68—The Electoral College   56

No. 70—The Presidency: Efficiency
  and Responsibility   59

No. 71—The Presidency: Term Length   65

No. 78—The Supreme Court   69

IV.   Appendices   76

      1. Key Quotations from the Original Text
         of *The Federalist*   76

      2. The Declaration of Independence   83

      3. The Articles of Confederation   87

      4. The U.S. Constitution   96

V.   Index   119

Acknowledgments

I would first like to thank Gary Glenn, a legendary teacher of American political thought at Northern Illinois University for the past half century. It was during the course of one of our usual morning conversations in the office at NIU that I became excited about the idea for this work, and it was while teaching a course he invented that I honed my ability to successfully undertake it. I benefited enormously from Gary's mentorship as a junior faculty member and will continue to draw on his example throughout my teaching career.

Many thanks are also due to Jim Read and an anonymous reviewer for their careful reading of the manuscript and for offering excellent suggestions for its improvement at various points throughout. Brian Rak provided outstanding editorial direction of the project from beginning to end. I take full responsibility for any errors that remain.

I.
Introduction

There was a time when the Constitution was not yet a historical document. There was a time before it had been subjected to the interpretation and reinterpretation of the Supreme Court over the course of hundreds of cases. There was a time when it looked doubtful that the people of the thirteen independent states would agree to a plan for a new federal government that had been produced in secrecy and without legal authorization.

It was at this time that Alexander Hamilton, James Madison, and John Jay wrote the newspaper articles that together would become *The Federalist*. They united under one name, Publius, and shared one purpose: to persuade the people of New York to support ratification of a new Constitution for the United States. This proposed Constitution was written and adopted by a convention of delegates appointed by individual states, a convention whose official purpose was to revise the existing Articles of Confederation. These delegates shared a justifiably urgent concern for the viability of the fledgling United States, and they quickly realized that their task of rescuing the United States required more than a simple revision of the Articles.

The Articles of Confederation had created a "league" or treaty between the states rather than a government for the nation like those in existence for each of the states. The states each had one vote in the Congress, and unanimity was required. The individual citizens of the states had no direct connection with the national government; they weren't represented within it, and they couldn't be directly acted upon by it. The Union that was created as a military alliance during the Revolutionary War continued to act as a mere alliance after the war was over. The United States under the Articles of Confederation was organized along the same lines as all preceding confederations in history, and it was destined to collapse in precisely the same way: through the inability of the central government to effectively coordinate national affairs.

Because of this, the Articles of Confederation needed to be entirely replaced. As Hamilton put it in *Federalist* 15, "the evils we experience do not proceed from minute or partial imperfections, but from fundamental errors in the structure of the building, which cannot be amended otherwise than by an alteration in the first principles and main pillars of the fabric." And Madison described the Constitutional Convention in *Federalist* 40 as "deeply and unanimously impressed with the crisis, which had led their country almost with one voice to make so singular and solemn an experiment for correcting the errors of a system by which this crisis had been produced." The structure of the federal union had to be entirely remade, and an essential part of this remaking was the formation of a national government with sufficient authority and power to counterbalance that of the individual states.

Despite their unanimous agreement on the necessity of adopting an entirely new Constitution, the convention delegates knew they would face a difficult battle in securing its ratification by the specially-elected state conventions. The people knew essentially nothing about the proposed Constitution until it was actually placed in front of them for their consideration. Something so novel in conception and momentous in importance would require all of the persuasive ability the convention delegates could muster for its support. It was far from certain that the Constitution would be ratified, and the efforts of Federalists such as the Publius authors would be absolutely crucial in bringing this about.

The Federalist differs, then, from most books of political philosophy not only in its multiple authorship but also in its direction to a definite practical purpose. Hamilton, Madison, and Jay each had their own distinct opinions about politics, and these opinions didn't always fit neatly together. And because they were engaged in a debate with very practical and even personal stakes, they had powerful motivation to bend their arguments to better serve their ultimate goals. The arguments presented in *The Federalist* are, in other words, delivered to us in far messier fashion than the stereotypical armchair utterances of the disinterested philosopher.

In the very first *Federalist* essay, Hamilton warns his readers that the arguments on both sides of the ratification debate are likely to be accompanied by a "false bias" brought about by "ambition, avarice, personal animosity, party opposition, and many other motives." He doesn't exempt himself from this sort of bias, even while being careful to heap more doubt upon his opponents' motivations than his own. In a sobering and brilliant commentary on the nature of public debate at this critical juncture in American—and indeed human—history, Hamilton deftly attempts to achieve some distance for himself and his coauthors from the obvious charge of bias that would naturally be leveled against them in their attempt to defend the proposed Constitution.

Despite Hamilton's efforts at the outset, though, many both at the time and since have tended to view the *Federalist* essays with some suspicion. After all, the two principal Publius authors—Hamilton and Madison—were leading figures in the convention that produced the proposed Constitution. In addition to possessing an intimate knowledge of the convention's deliberations, they would have had strong feelings of attachment to it and responsibility for its success. All three of the Publius authors would go on to hold prestigious political positions in the new political order inaugurated by the Constitution: Hamilton as secretary of the Treasury, Madison as a member of the House of Representatives, secretary of state, and president, and Jay as the first chief justice of the U.S. Supreme Court. Given all of this, it is difficult to deny the workings of some measure of "false bias" in Publius' essays.

This undeniably practical and rhetorical context of *The Federalist* suggests its value as a historical document. As a historical document, it can shed light on the issues and debates of the time, as well as the thoughts and motivations of the participants in these debates. It can help us to understand what was important to the Americans of the time, how they viewed their political situation, and how some of the key political figures of the founding era shaped the direction of early American politics. It can help us to appreciate the rich context within which the U.S. Constitution was written, considered, and adopted.

Madison's *Federalist* 39 provides an excellent example of this. The essay clearly reveals the importance of three political concepts at the time: republicanism, federalism, and nationalism. It also illustrates how these concepts were understood, both singly and in balance with one another, by Madison and his contemporaries. Far from a philosophical treatise on these concepts, it showcases the extent of Madison's excellent rhetorical abilities in navigating his argument for the Constitution through the minefield of political opinions at the time.

Republicanism is depicted in the essay as an essential component of "the genius of the people of America." Almost everyone on almost all sides of political questions in America at the time viewed themselves as a "republican." The Constitution couldn't be adopted if it failed to follow this republican predisposition of the American people. But if the commitment to republicanism itself wasn't a matter for debate, its meaning certainly was. Madison shows the "extreme inaccuracy with which the term has been used" and provides a new definition of republicanism that, not surprisingly, fits the proposed Constitution very well. Here, then, we have a discussion that is revealing both of the state of common opinion at the time, and of Madison's particular attempt at clarifying and sharpening that common opinion in a manner that agrees with the understanding that produced the new Constitution.

In the case of federalism and nationalism, Madison appears to be navigating a difficult tightrope between two relatively well-defined political positions at the time: those who emphasize the need for a more "energetic" national government than the one authorized by the Articles of Confederation, and those who emphasize the importance of maintaining the Articles' arrangement regarding the sovereignty and independence of the states. The former tend to be "Federalists" in support of the proposed Constitution, and include Hamilton and Madison among their prominent leaders; the latter tend to be "Anti-Federalists" in opposition to the proposed Constitution. By carefully arguing that the proposed Constitution is "neither a national nor a federal" one, Madison is attempting to steer a middle path that will assuage the concerns of some Anti-Federalists without betraying those of his Federalist allies.

Federalist 39 has much to teach us about the time in which it was written: about the opinions that Madison and others held, about the debates in which they were engaged, and about the political circumstances within which they lived. But this essay might also contain the potential to help us reflect upon our own time and political circumstances as well.

Our world today isn't identical to Publius' in 1787, but neither is it wholly different from it. Many of the debates that were particularly controversial at the time of the Constitution continue to be controversial today. Issues of minority rights, the responsibility of government to the people, states' rights versus federal authority, political equality, and race relations occupied political actors at the time of the founding just as they occupy us today. The concepts, approaches, and arguments they utilized, along with the concrete circumstances within which these issues were manifested, might indeed differ in important ways from our own. These differences, though, can be sources of illumination rather than alienation.

Publius viewed the Constitution as a "reflection on human nature,"[1] and as the embodiment both of a realistic assessment of "the infirmities and depravities of the human character"[2] and of a moral vision deriving in large part from the "principles of the Revolution"[3] as enunciated in the Declaration of Independence. Throughout *The Federalist*, Publius

---

1   *Federalist* 51.

2   *Federalist* 37.

3   *Federalist* 39.

is frequently concerned with showing how the proposed Constitution effectively takes this twofold understanding of human nature into account. In *Federalist* 10, for example, Madison is concerned with the manner in which the problem of "factions" should influence constitutional design. He defines factions as kinds of interest groups whose agendas are inimical to the rights of other citizens or to the aggregate interests of the community. The fact that factions exist at all is a direct consequence of human nature in the form of its "infirmities and depravities." Wherever there is liberty there will be factions, and "the latent causes of faction" are inextricably "sown in the nature of man." This point emerges prominently again in *Federalist* 51, where the conflictual model of ambition counteracting ambition becomes necessary due to "the defect of better motives" such as respect for others and a disinterested concern for the good of the whole society.

The fact that factions represent a serious problem to be controlled, on the other hand, follows from an understanding of human nature in the form of the moral vision it includes. Factions arise out of a condition of liberty but tend to destroy this liberty through their opposition to the rights of others and the common goods of the whole society. These rights and common goods are those paradigmatically expressed in the Declaration's account of the origin and purposes of government: the rights of "life, liberty and the pursuit of happiness," and the common goods of "safety and happiness." It is human nature, as it becomes attached to us through our creation by "Nature's God," which reveals the outlines and components of the moral vision that is reflected in the Constitution's design and that guides Publius' defense of it in *The Federalist*.

The dynamic interplay of these two faces of human nature is reflected in the framers' search for what Madison famously describes in *Federalist* 10 as "a republican remedy for the diseases most incident to republican government." The Revolutionary principles of natural rights, as well as those "qualities in human nature which justify a certain portion of esteem and confidence,"[4] point in the direction of what Madison terms a "pure democracy." This is why the state constitutions created during the Revolution and following on the heels of the Declaration were overwhelmingly democratic in nature.

The examples of democratic state politics confirmed, however, what the history of democracies suggested: that too-pure democracies tend to be "spectacles of turbulence and contention," and "incompatible with

---

4   *Federalist* 55.

personal security or the rights of property."[5] This results from the second, less auspicious face of human nature: the "degree of depravity in mankind which requires a certain degree of circumspection and distrust."[6] In *Federalist* 10, Madison masterfully attempts to show how the design of the proposed Constitution as an "extended republic" properly reflects the complex tension between the two sides of human nature.

Because this two-sided human nature doesn't seem to have changed much between Publius' time and our own, a dialogue between Publius and ourselves appears possible. And because such a dialogue is possible, it is, in fact, required of any search for an accurate and genuine historical understanding of *The Federalist*. The framers and defenders of the Constitution were engaged in activities with which we can relate and sympathize, and they had opinions and made arguments related to these activities in precisely the same way we do today. If we nevertheless treat their opinions, arguments, and actions as things alien and ossified, we fail to understand and appreciate them as they actually existed at the time. Unless we attempt to put ourselves in their shoes, or in the shoes of someone actually interacting with the authors at the time in which they wrote, we fall short of understanding the past as it really existed.

In other words, although *The Federalist* is indeed a historical document that emerged from and was directed to a particular time period with particular concerns, historical sensitivity itself should also lead one to view *The Federalist* as something more than this. Because it wasn't a historical document at the time in which it was written, defended, and adopted, to view it only as such is to preclude authentic understanding and appreciation. And without an authentic understanding and appreciation for Publius' opinions and arguments, we may miss the opportunity to benefit from his reflections and insights regarding issues that we continue to struggle with today.

It is often thought that to treat a historical text in this way is to use history as a means in the service of our own particular ends, and thereby to distort rather than faithfully understand the original. Because the authors existed *within* a certain historical context, it seems that to ignore this contextual difference is to fail to take an essential component of the historical text into account. It is equally important, though, to appreciate the fact that the authors of such a text *existed* within a certain historical context—that they interacted with their world in the same way, broadly speaking, that we

---

5   *Federalist* 10.
6   *Federalist* 55.

interact with ours. Unless their world has nothing at all in common with ours, this sort of appreciation is essential to historical understanding.

Nor are these two perspectives mutually exclusive. Historical authors and their texts aren't objects entirely alien to us; nor do they exist in some abstract ahistorical ether. Historical authors and their texts had as real an existence as we enjoy now; the circumstances surrounding their existence were, though, different in various and variable ways from our own. It is with these ideas in mind that the following version of *The Federalist* proceeds. It is intended to be a supplement to, rather than a substitute for, the original version. The original version remains essential to achieving the many aspects of historical understanding already mentioned. The new version that follows, on the other hand, is designed to supply what is now missing from the original for the vast majority of readers: the ability to connect, engage, and dialogue with Publius' thought processes and arguments.

The original language and style of *The Federalist*, though frequently beautiful and striking, is so different from our own as to render understanding very difficult even for academics and professors. Sometimes the fault lies in our inferior prowess in expression and comprehension today, sometimes it lies in the simple extinction over time of particular words and idioms, and sometimes it lies in unfortunate idiosyncrasies of expression during Publius' time. Whatever the reason or combination of reasons, the fact is that most—and perhaps nearly all—of us are no longer able to access a good portion of the original ideas, opinions, and arguments in *The Federalist* through the original text.

This new version is intended to make the most important ideas and arguments in *The Federalist* accessible to ordinary citizens today. Care has been taken to only depart from the original text for the sake of accessibility to modern readers, and not for the sake of interpretation. My aim hasn't been to improve upon or even to clarify the original text, but only to faithfully transmit its meaning to a current-day audience for whom the original is too often impenetrable. It is intended to be a scholarly translation rather than an updating or a dumbing-down of the original.

In such a task, though, some loss of nuance and connotation is inevitable. There are, moreover, certain to be points at which I have fallen short of conveying the precise meaning of the original through my own particular failing. In an effort to make up for these shortcomings, I have included an appendix of key quotations from the original text of *The Federalist*. And for whatever deficiencies remain, I offer my apologies to the original authors and hope that they will be more inclined to applaud my effort than to condemn my presumption.

II.

A Note on the Text

A significant portion of the unusual sort of translation attempted herein consisted in rendering Publius' unwieldy, multiple-clause sentences digestible for the modern reader with the minimum amount of alteration. Most often this involved making one sentence into two or three, along with the correspondingly necessary minor alterations in phrasing. Occasionally, when leaving a lengthy sentence intact seemed desirable for the purpose of preserving Publius' meaning, this involved numbering the clauses within it for increased ease of organization and comprehension.

Another significant task consisted in finding modern equivalents for words and phrases used by Publius that are no longer understood by most readers. In *Federalist* 10 and elsewhere, for example, Publius uses the term "popular government" to mean something very different from what we, in the days of polls and popularity ratings, might mean by this. What he means is something closer to "government based on the people," and it is this formulation that I have decided—at the excellent suggestion of one of the manuscript's readers—to adopt in place of the original, now misleading one.

There is a spectrum along which Publius' unfamiliar words and phrases fall, from ones that are uncommon but still understandable by the average American to ones that most scholars would need to investigate to understand accurately. If I judged an uncommon word or phrase to be understandable by an average undergraduate student, I retained it. If such a student would likely not understand the word or phrase accurately, I replaced it with the closest available modern equivalent. One advantage of translating from an earlier to a later form of the same language is that there tend to be close equivalents available in almost all cases.

For my source text I used the original McLean edition of 1788, which is generally recognized as authentic. The italicization of the original text was generally retained, as was the occasional capitalization of entire words. Direct quotations have also been retained without alteration. The superscript numbers indicate that the original version of the immediately preceding text is provided in Appendix 1.

My general operative principle was to make only the minimum alterations necessary to the original text to render it understandable by the average unaided undergraduate. Sometimes this principle indicated extensive departures from the original, and sometimes the original is left completely untouched. My goal was to preserve the reader's sense that he or she was reading the words of Publius, simply in a form that was now much more readily accessible.

III.

The Federalist Papers

Federalist 1

[Hamilton]

After a clear experience of the inefficiency of the existing federal government, you are now called upon to consider a new Constitution for the United States of America. The importance of this task is obvious. The very existence of the Union, the safety and welfare of the parts composing it, and the fate of the developing American empire depend upon it. It has often been said that the conduct and example of the American people may answer an important question for mankind: Are societies capable of establishing good government from their own reflection and choice, or are they forever destined to have governments imposed upon them through chance and violence?[1] If there is any truth to this opinion, now is the time when our answer will be given. If we fail to make the right choice, our failure may deserve to be considered the general misfortune of mankind.

This adds the motive of philanthropy to that of patriotism in leading responsible and good citizens to care deeply about this task of considering the Constitution. Although I hope that our decision will be guided by a balanced estimate of our true interests, this is more a wish than an expectation. The proposed Constitution affects too many particular interests and changes too many local institutions. As a result of this, discussions of the proposed Constitution will often involve a variety of topics irrelevant to its merits, and will reflect many views, passions, and prejudices opposed to the discovery of truth.

One of the most difficult obstacles the new Constitution will encounter will be the obvious interest of many state-level politicians and officials in resisting any change which might diminish their power. Then there is also the misguided ambition of those who will try to take advantage of general political instability for their own gain, or try to encourage the formation of partial confederacies of states in the hope of wielding more political power than they would within a single, larger Union.

I do not, however, intend to dwell upon the potentially selfish motives of those who are opposed to the Constitution. It would be wrong to dismiss anyone's opposition as the result of narrow interest or ambition. Even those who oppose the new Constitution may be influenced by respectable motives and merely be guilty of honest errors. Our judgment is so frequently biased by numerous causes that we often see wise and good men on the wrong side of important questions for society. This should teach all of us to be civil in our disagreements with each other, no matter how convinced we are that we are in the right.

Another reason for caution in our disagreements is that we are not always sure that those who argue for the truth are any more pure in their motives than their opponents. Ambition, greed, personal animosity, party politics, and many other discreditable motives are just as capable of affecting those on the right side of a question as those on the wrong side. Even if these reasons for civility and caution didn't exist, the intolerant spirit which always characterizes political parties would still be extremely imprudent. For in politics, as in religion, it is equally absurd to aim at making converts by fire and sword. Heresies in either can rarely be cured by persecution.

And yet, however convincing these reasons are, we already have enough of an indication that this great national discussion of the Constitution will not be any different from other national discussions. A torrent of angry and malicious passions will be let loose. Both sides will try to win the argument and persuade others to their position by shouting down and insulting the other. An appropriate concern for the energy and efficiency of government will be stigmatized as a fondness for despotic power and a hostility to the principles of liberty. An excessive worry about potential dangers to the rights of the people, which usually shows that one's heart is in the right place even if the worry is mistaken, will be misrepresented as a mere popularity stunt. It will be forgotten, on the one hand, that a noble love for liberty is often accompanied by a suspicious distrust of power. On the other hand, it will be equally forgotten that the power of government is essential to the security of liberty. It will be forgotten, also, that dangers to liberty more often lurk behind the mask of zeal for the rights of the people than under an open endorsement of the energy and efficiency of government. History teaches us that the former has been found a much more certain road to the introduction of tyranny and oppression than the latter, and that the greatest number of tyrants began by catering to the people.

I have said all of this with a view to putting you, my fellow citizens, on your guard against those who might attempt to influence your decision on this important matter by any means other than an objective presentation of the evidence. At the same time, you have probably gathered that I myself am disposed in favor of the new Constitution. Yes, fellow citizens, I admit to you that, after considering the matter very carefully, I am clearly of the opinion that it is in your interest to adopt it. I am convinced that this is the safest course for your liberty, your dignity, and your happiness. I will not pretend to be undecided. I openly acknowledge my convictions, and I will freely explain the reasons for these convictions to you. Since my intentions are genuine, I have no desire to be ambiguous. My arguments will be open to all, and may be judged by all. They will at least be offered in the spirit of discovering the truth.

I propose, in a series of papers, to discuss the following points in particular:

(1) The utility of the Union to your political prosperity.

(2) The insufficiency of the existing government under the Articles of Confederation to preserve that Union.

(3) The necessity of a government at least as efficient as the one in the proposed Constitution to effectively preserve the Union.

(4) The conformity of the proposed Constitution to the true principles of republican government.

(5) The similarities of the proposed Constitution to your own state constitution.

(6) And finally, the additional security which its adoption will provide for the preservation of the state governments, for liberty, and for property.

I will also attempt to answer any important objections which may arise during the time that I am writing these papers.

Some may think there is no need to give arguments showing the utility of the Union, because recent experience has already made this clear to everyone. The fact is, however, that many who oppose the new Constitution are already spreading the idea that a union of all thirteen states will be too large, and that a number of smaller unions including fewer states will be preferable to one Union including all. This shows the real alternative we have in front of us: an adoption of the new Constitution or a breaking apart of the Union. It will, therefore, be useful to begin by examining the advantages of the Union, as well as the certain evils and probable dangers to states which would result from its dissolution. This will, accordingly, constitute the subject of my next paper.

Federalist 10

[Madison]

The ability of a well-constructed union to control the negative effects of factions is perhaps its most important advantage. Everywhere in the world and throughout history, the problem of factions has proven to be the downfall of governments based on the people. It is true that widespread political participation can lead to instability, injustice, and confusion in government. These have been the mortal diseases under which governments based on the people have generally perished, and they provide the enemies of liberty with easy ammunition for their arguments. If, then, the union proposed by the Constitution contains a solution to the problem of factions that still remains faithful to the idea of government by the people, this would be a crucial point in its favor.

The state constitutions have certainly made significant improvements upon historical models of government by the people. The states have, however, failed to solve the crucial problem of factions. This has been made clear by the complaints of upstanding citizens in many of the states that their governments are unstable, that the public good is lost in the conflict between competing parties, and that the majority is often able to use public policy to violate the rules of justice and the rights of the minority. These complaints are, moreover, supported by known facts. Although it is true that some of them may refer to problems caused by other, non-governmental sources, it is clear that the worst of these problems—especially the growing lack of faith in government and the widespread fear for the security of individual rights—is in fact due to the influence of factions in the operation of our state governments.

By *faction* I mean a group of citizens—whether or not they add up to a majority—united and driven by particular interests or passions that are opposed either to the rights of other citizens or to the long-term and common interests of the community.[1] There are only two ways of preventing these factions from causing the problems mentioned above: (1) removing the *causes* of factions; and (2) controlling their *effects*.

There are two ways of removing the *causes* of factions: the first is to suppress individual liberty, and the second is to give all individuals the same opinions, passions, and interests. Pursuing the first—suppressing individual liberty—would be worse than simply allowing factions to flourish. Factions need liberty for their existence, just as fire needs air. And it would be just as ridiculous to eliminate liberty for the sake of preventing factions as it would be to eliminate air for the sake of preventing fire.[2]

Pursuing the second—giving everyone the same opinions, passions, and interests—is simply impracticable. As long as people are free to think for themselves and capable of making mistakes in their thinking, they will form different opinions. As long as people tend to prefer themselves to others, their self-centered passions will attach to and intensify their opinions, and vice versa. Giving everyone the same interests is similarly impracticable because differences in interests are primarily defined by differences in the amounts and kinds of property people possess, and these differences in property ownership are determined by different and unequal uses of individual liberty. Because the protection of individual liberty is the primary goal of government,[3] differences in property ownership and, therefore, differences in interests will necessarily exist in a free society.

The causes of faction are simply a part of human nature, and that is why factions appear in all political societies to whatever extent circumstances allow. The strength of people's attachments to their different opinions regarding religion and politics, including personal attachments to certain politicians or public figures, makes them generally much more willing to argue than to cooperate for the common good. This tendency is so strong that people will often find the most meaningless or superficial excuses to argue and fight with each other. There is, though, one main source of conflict that has always divided citizens against one another, and this is the unequal distribution of wealth. The rich and the poor have always formed different interests in society. In any advanced nation a variety of different and unequal economic interests are bound to develop, and these economic interests will strongly influence opinions and emotions. Modern lawmaking is primarily concerned with regulating these different and conflicting interests, which means that factions have a necessary place in the day-to-day operation of government.

We don't allow any individual citizen to be the judge in their own case, because their self-interest would make them biased. But aren't representatives in a legislature in a similar position, just on a larger scale? Aren't laws determinations of the rights of large groups of citizens who are represented in the legislature, which means that representatives are judges in their own case as much as an individual citizen would be? Justice usually lies between opposing sides on questions of public policy. But the parties to each side are the only available judges, and the most numerous party—or the most powerful faction—normally wins. Neither of the parties deciding a question of public policy can be expected to do so on the basis of justice and the common good. In fact, the very issues which often require the most impartiality to be decided correctly—such as taxation—are the ones where bias and unfairness tend to be the most prevalent.

Nor should we simply hope for great leaders who will rise above these partisan clashes and inspire a united commitment to the public good. Such leaders will not always be available.[4] And even when they are, the attachment of opposing parties to their immediate interests at the expense of long-term interests would still pose a significant obstacle to their efforts.

The conclusion we are led to is that the first method of controlling factions mentioned above—removing their *causes*—is impossible. The only remaining option for dealing with factions is, then, the second mentioned: controlling their *effects*.

Since our proposed government will be based on the people, minority factions will not ordinarily pose the most serious problems. In a government based on the people, the majority that opposes a minority faction has the available means to defeat it by simply voting it down. A majority faction, on the other hand, has the ability in such a government to sacrifice both the public good and the rights of minorities to its own interests. The great task we have before us then is this: to protect the public good and the rights of minorities from the power of a majority faction without abandoning the idea of government by the people. This is the only way that we can rescue the worldwide reputation of this kind of government and show mankind that it is viable.[5]

How can this task be accomplished? It seems there are only two ways: we must either (1) somehow prevent the same emotion or interest from existing in a majority at the same time; or (2) if the majority do have the same emotion or interest at the same time, they must be prevented in some way from uniting and using this emotion or interest as an excuse to oppress a minority. If the motive and the opportunity are both present, we know that neither religious nor moral influences can be counted on to restrain an oppressive majority. Such influences are not normally effective in restraining individuals, and their effectiveness tends to decrease even further in the case of groups.

From this it is clear that a pure democracy—a small society where the government consists of all of the citizens meeting in person—has no way to prevent the problems of faction. The majority will have the same emotion or interest in almost every case, and there is nothing to stop them from sacrificing a minority or an individual for the sake of this emotion or interest. This is why pure democracies have always been unstable, dangerous to personal security and property rights, short-lived, and prone to violent destruction. Political theorists who have favored this type of government have mistakenly thought that by ensuring equality in political rights they could also count on similarity in citizens' property, opinions, and emotions.

A republic, on the other hand—a government based on the people but involving representation—does promise the cure for the problems of faction that we are looking for. If we notice the ways in which a republic differs from a pure democracy, we will see both the nature of the cure and the usefulness of the Union when compared with the states.

There are two main differences between a pure democracy and a republic: (1) in a republic, government is the job of a small number of citizens elected by the people, rather than the whole people itself; and (2) a republic may be extended over a much larger population and territory.

The first difference has two possible effects. On the one hand, the small number of citizens elected by the people might be wiser and more dedicated to the common good than the average citizen. This would give them the ability to filter and broaden the views of their constituents.[6] As a result of this, public policy might be much better under a republic than it would be under a pure democracy, where the views of the people aren't filtered and broadened in this way. On the other hand, though, the opposite might be the case as well. Ambitious citizens with bad intentions may be elected through false campaigning or corruption, and then betray the interests of the people once they are in office. The question is whether small or large republics are more likely to result in good representatives.

The answer to this question is clearly in favor of large ones, for two reasons: (1) First, in any republic, the number of representatives has to be high enough to guard against possible conspiracies that may arise among a small group, but also low enough to allow for productive discussion and decision-making. Because the number of representatives needs to be determined in this way rather than simply in proportion to the size of the nation, the proportion of representatives to citizens will be greater in a small republic than in a large one. And if the proportion of worthy candidates to average citizens is the same in both, there will be a greater number of such candidates in a large republic than in a small one. This will increase the probability of worthy candidates being elected to serve as representatives in a large republic.

Secondly (2), false campaigning should be more difficult in a large republic since there are more people to deceive. Candidates will have to be more honest with more people watching them, which will result in elections based primarily on the merit and character of the candidates.

There is, however, a happy medium when it comes to the size of a republic. If it is too big, the representatives will be too unfamiliar with their constituents; if it is too small, the representatives will be too attached to their particular constituents and not attached enough to the common good of the whole nation. The proposed Constitution finds this happy medium by assigning the tasks relating to the common interests of the whole nation to the national Congress, and the tasks relating to local and particular interests to the state legislatures.

The other main difference between a republic and a pure democracy is that a republic may be extended over a much larger population and territory. This difference is the main reason why republics possess the cure for the problems of faction which always destroy pure democracies. The smaller the population and territory of a nation, the less variety there will be in the interests of the people. The less variety there is in the interests of the people, the more likely it will be that a majority will be united by the same interest against a minority, and the easier it will be for this majority to coordinate with each other to further this interest at the expense of the minority. Extend the sphere—make the population and territory of a society much larger—and there will be a greater variety of interests present in the society. The more interests are present, the less likely it will be that a majority will form around a single interest that is opposed to the rights of a minority.[7] And even if such an interest were present, it would be more difficult for a larger number of citizens to realize this fact and effectively unite with each other to oppress a minority. Communicating unfair and selfish purposes requires a certain amount of trust, and such trust is not likely to be felt among a large group of citizens extending over a large territory.

Therefore it seems clear that the same advantages which a republic has over a pure democracy in preventing the problems of faction are also possessed by a large republic over a small one—in other words, by the Union over the states.[8] These advantages consist both in (1) representatives who are more likely to be dedicated to the common good, and in (2) the greater security to minorities that results from the greater variety of interests. Taking these together, there will be much greater obstacles to the oppression of a minority by the majority in the Union than in the states.

The influence of a narrow interest might be strong within a single state, but it will be unlikely to spread through the other states. A religious sect might gain political power in one state, but the variety of religious sects throughout the Union will prevent any one of them from gaining political power in the national government. Movements for the radical redistribution of property or other particular economic interests will also be less likely to spread throughout the Union than to be present in a particular state, just as such particular interests are more likely to be powerful in a county or district than in an entire state.

In the size and structure of the Union, therefore, we have found a solution to the problem of factions that remains faithful to the idea of government by the people.[9] Insofar as we cherish this form of government, we should support the adoption of the proposed Constitution for our Union.

Federalist 14

[Madison]

We have seen the necessity of the Union from many angles: (1) as our protection against foreign enemies; (2) as keeping peace among the states; (3) as coordinating commerce and other common interests; (4) as the only substitute for permanent standing armies in the states, which are dangerous to civil liberties; and (5) as the cure for the diseases of faction, which have been fatal to other governments based on the people and which have begun to infect our own. The last topic to consider along these lines is whether, as some have said, the territory of the United States is simply too large for a government based on the people.

I have already explained why it is wrong to assume that government based on the people can only occur in a small territory. I will add here that this error seems to stem from the common confusion of a republic with a pure democracy, applying arguments to republics that only hold true for pure democracies. As I have already explained (*Federalist* 10), the difference between these forms of government is that, in a pure democracy, the people meet and exercise the government in person; while in a republic, they exercise the government through representatives. A pure democracy, therefore, is only possible over a small territory. A republic, on the other hand, may be extended over a large one.[1]

Some famous and influential authors have also contributed to this error. Being subjects of kings, they have attempted to make monarchies look better by comparing them to the worst historical examples of government by the people. Because of the similar meanings of *republic*—public government—and *democracy*—rule by the people—it has been easy to transfer observations about pure democracies to republics, including the observation that it can only be established in a small territory.

Another reason this mistake hasn't been sufficiently noticed is that examples of unmixed republics are very difficult to find. In the ancient world, most of the governments based on the people were pure democracies, and in modern Europe—where the principle of representation was discovered—there are no governments based entirely on the people and operating entirely through representation. If Europe claims the distinction of discovering this great mechanical power in government which can concentrate the will of the largest population and direct its force to any object required for the public good, America claims the distinction of making this discovery the basis of unmixed republics extending over a large territory. It is only unfortunate that any American citizen should want to deprive her of the additional distinction of showing the full effectiveness of the principle of representation in the establishment of the constitutional system now under consideration.

The natural territorial limit of a pure democracy is that distance from the center which will just allow the most remote citizens to assemble as often as their public functions demand, and the natural population limit is the number of citizens who can join in those functions. The natural limit of a republic, on the other hand, is that distance from the center which will just allow the representatives to meet as often as may be necessary for the administration of public affairs. Do the limits of the United States exceed this distance? Considering our experience over the last thirteen years, it seems not. The Atlantic coast is the longest side of the Union, and during these last thirteen years the representatives of the states have been almost continually assembled. The representatives from the most distant states have not, though, been absent from Congress any more than those from the states nearest to the capital.

So that we can have a more precise estimate with regard to this interesting subject, let us consider the actual dimensions of the Union. The territorial boundaries, as determined by the treaty of peace, are: on the east the Atlantic, on the south the latitude of 31 degrees, on the west the Mississippi River, and on the north a crooked line running between the latitudes of 45 and 42 degrees. The distance between the 31st and 45th degrees (the longest south–north distance) is 973 miles, and the distance between the 31st and 42nd degrees (the shortest south–north distance) is 764.5 miles. The average south–north distance is, therefore, 868.75 miles.

The average east–west distance from the Atlantic to the Mississippi is probably less than 750 miles. Comparing these dimensions with those of several European countries, it seems clear that this is not too large of a territory for the representative principle to operate. It is not much larger than Germany, where an assembly representing the whole empire is continually gathered. Nor is it much larger than Poland, which possessed a similar assembly. Although Great Britain is smaller, the representatives of the northern tip of the island have as far to travel to the national council as will those of the most remote parts of the Union.

There are, moreover, further reasons supporting the possibility of extending representation over the whole territory of the Union.

First, the general government of the Union will not have the whole power of making and enforcing laws. Its jurisdiction is, rather, limited to certain enumerated objects which concern the entire republic but cannot be accomplished by any of the states separately. The lower levels of government, which are able to efficiently deal with those objects which can be accomplished separately, will keep their appropriate authority and power. If the new Constitution proposed to abolish the state governments, its opponents would have some basis for their objection. And even if the state governments were abolished, it would be easy to show that the general government of the Union would be forced to reinstate them in order to preserve itself.

A second observation to be made is that the immediate goal of the new Constitution is to secure the union of the thirteen original states, which we already know to be possible, and to add to them the other states that may arise either out of their existing territories or in their immediate vicinity, which would seem equally possible. The arrangements that may be necessary for those parts of our territory which lie on our northwestern frontier must be left to others at a future time.

Thirdly, it should be noted that travel throughout the Union will be made easier by new improvements. Roads will be shortened and better maintained, there will be more and better accommodations for travelers, and an interior navigation on our eastern side will be opened throughout the whole length of the thirteen states. Transportation between the western and Atlantic districts, as well as within each, will be made increasingly easy by the numerous canals which nature has given us and which our effort completes.

A fourth and even more important consideration follows from the fact that almost every state will, on one side or another, be a frontier, and will thus benefit from the protection of the Union. The states that are farthest from the center of the Union—and which might, then, receive a lesser share of its ordinary benefits—will be immediately bordering foreign nations, and will therefore occasionally stand in the greatest need of the Union's strength and resources. It may be inconvenient for Georgia, or the states forming our western or northeastern borders, to send their representatives to the capital, but it would be even more inconvenient for them to bear the entire military and financial burden of defending themselves against invading enemies. Therefore, even if they will receive less benefits from the Union in some respects than the less distant states, they will receive greater benefits in other ways.

I share these thoughts with you, my fellow citizens, knowing that your good judgment will take them into proper consideration; and that you will never allow apparently formidable difficulties based upon common errors to drive you to the gloomy conclusions argued by the advocates for disunion. Do not listen to those who say that the people of America, knit together as they are by so many threads of affection, can no longer live together as members of the same family; can no longer continue the mutual guardians of their mutual happiness; can no longer be fellow citizens of one great, respectable, and thriving empire. Do not listen to those who say that the form of government in the proposed Constitution has never been tried before; that it has never been considered even by the wildest imaginations; that it attempts to accomplish the impossible. No, my countrymen, shut your ears against this evil language. Shut your hearts against the poison which it carries. The common blood which flows in the veins of American citizens, the same blood which they have shed in defense of their sacred rights, consecrates their Union and inspires horror at the idea of their becoming foreigners, competitors, and enemies.

And if new political experiments are to be avoided, believe me, the most dangerous and rash of all is that of tearing us in pieces in order to preserve our liberty and promote our happiness. But why should the experiment of an extended republic be rejected simply because it is new and untried? It is, after all, the glory of the people of America that, while they have respected the opinions of the past and of other nations, they have not allowed a blind veneration for these opinions to override the influence of their own good judgment, the knowledge of their own situation, and the lessons of their own experience. Future generations of Americans, and indeed the whole world, will be indebted to us for the numerous innovations we have displayed in favor of private rights and public happiness.[2] If the leaders of the Revolution had been careful not to take any unprecedented step, and not to establish any untried form of government, the people of the United States might at this very moment have been suffering under the oppression of one of those forms of government which have crushed the liberties of the rest of mankind. Happily for America, and happily for the whole human race, they pursued a new and more noble course. They accomplished a revolution which has no parallel in human history. They constructed governments which have no model on the face of the globe.[3] They formed the design of a great Confederation, which their successors are obligated to improve and perpetuate. If they have made mistakes, we are surprised at how few there are. If they made the most mistakes in the structure of the Union under the Articles of Confederation, this was the task most difficult to execute. It is this task which has been attempted again by the Constitutional Convention, and it is this attempt which you are now asked to judge and decide upon.

Federalist 15

[Hamilton]

In the preceding papers I have attempted, my fellow citizens, to clearly and convincingly set forth the importance of Union to your political safety and happiness. I have shown you the dangers that would follow from allowing the sacred tie which binds the people of America together to be broken by ambition, greed, jealousy, or misrepresentation. In the coming papers, the points I have made will be further supported by new facts and arguments. If the journey through these papers seems boring or bothersome at times, you should remember three things: (1) that you are in search of information on the most important subject which can concern a free people, (2) that the field of relevant information and arguments through which you are traveling is a very large one, and (3) that the journey has been made unnecessarily difficult by the mazes which have been set up by false arguments. I will attempt to remove the obstacles from your progress as briefly as I can without overlooking anything essential.

The next planned topic for discussion is the "insufficiency of the existing Confederation to the preservation of the Union." Why, though, should we take the trouble to argue a point which everyone, opponents and friends of the new Constitution alike, seems to admit already?

However much they disagree on other issues, both the opponents and friends of the new Constitution agree that something must be done to remedy the significant imperfections in our national system and rescue us from impending anarchy. The facts that support this common opinion are undeniable. They have been recognized by the people at large, and have finally led even those who are most responsible for our unfortunate situation to confess that our federal government does in fact possess serious defects—defects which have long been pointed out by the intelligent friends of the Union.

We have, indeed, reached almost the last stage of national humiliation. We have experienced nearly everything that can injure the pride or degrade the standing of an independent nation. We have constantly violated our obligations to other nations. We have been unable to repay the debts to foreigners and to our own citizens that allowed us to preserve our political existence in a time of extreme danger. We have allowed valuable territories and important posts to continue in the possession of a foreign power despite our own rights and interests in them. This has occurred because we have neither the troops, nor the treasury, nor the government to enable us to repel the aggression. Nor can we even complain of this aggression, because we ourselves have violated this same treaty. We have been excluded by Spain from navigating the Mississippi River, which we are entitled to do both by nature and by agreement. We seem to have abandoned all hope for public credit, which is an essential resource in times of public danger. Our commerce, which contributes greatly to national wealth, is at the lowest point of decline. Respectability among foreign powers is a safeguard against foreign encroachments, and foreign powers do not have enough respect for our government to even deal with us at all. The value of improved land in most parts of the country is surprisingly low, which can only fully be explained by a general and alarming lack of public confidence. Private credit as it relates to borrowing and lending, which is the friend and patron of industry, has contracted as a result not of the scarcity of money, but of an opinion of insecurity. In sum, despite the fact that we are uniquely blessed with natural advantages, we have nevertheless fallen prey to every conceivable national disorder, poverty, and insignificance.

This is the sad situation to which we have been brought by the very same political advice which now urges against the adoption of the proposed Constitution. Not content with having led us to the edge of a cliff, its proponents seem resolved to push us into the abyss that awaits us below. We should now, my countrymen, make a firm stand for our safety, peace, dignity, and reputation. We should break free of the temptation to follow entrenched opinions that lead us away from the path of happiness and prosperity.

It is true that undeniable facts have led both opponents and friends of the new Constitution to agree that there are significant imperfections in our national system. This agreement is useless, however, as long as the opponents of increased federal authority stubbornly oppose a remedy based upon the only principles that can give such a remedy a chance of success. While they admit that the government of the United States lacks the ability to efficiently accomplish its proper aims, they argue against giving it the powers which are necessary to supply that ability. They still seem to aim at mutually exclusive things: at an increase of federal authority without a decrease in state authority, and at a sovereignty in the Union along with a complete independence in the member states. They still, in short, seem to blindly value the nonsensical idea of an *imperium in imperio*—of one sovereign authority existing within another sovereign authority. This makes a full explanation of the primary defects of the Confederation necessary. Such an explanation will show that the evils we experience do not result from small or partial imperfections, but from fundamental errors in the structure of the whole system, and that these errors cannot be fixed unless we change the first principles and main pillars of this system.

The fundamental error in the construction of the existing Confederation is in the principle of making laws for states or governments as political units rather than for the individual citizens within them.[1] Though this principle does not run through all the powers given to the Union, it affects its most crucial ones. For example, the United States has the power to raise troops and money from the states, but it has no authority to directly raise them by making laws extending to the individual citizens of America. As a result of this, although in theory the resolutions of the United States concerning these matters are laws that constitutionally obligate the member states, in practice they are mere recommendations which the states follow or ignore at their discretion.

It is a clear example of the carelessness of the human mind that there are still those who object to the new Constitution because it departs from a principle which, as all experience has shown, was the downfall of the old one, and which is in itself obviously incompatible with the idea of government in general. The idea of government essentially involves replacing a resort to violence with regular political processes, and the principle of making laws for states or governments as political units is one which can only be enforced in practice through violent military conflict.

There is nothing absurd or impossible in the idea of an alliance between independent nations for particular purposes. These purposes may be precisely stated in a treaty which lays out the details of the alliance in advance and depends for its execution on the good faith of the parties to it. Alliances of this kind exist among all nations, frequently changing along with the shifting conditions of peace and war, and of observance and violation, in accordance with the interests of the parties. In the early part of this century these kinds of alliances were extremely popular, and politicians hoped for benefits from them which were never realized. In their attempt to establish the benefits of a balance of power and peace in Europe, every diplomatic resource was exhausted and triple and quadruple alliances were formed. The fact that these alliances were broken almost as soon as they were formed gave an important, though unfortunate, lesson to mankind: treaties that depend only on good faith, and that pit general considerations of peace and justice against particular interests, cannot be depended upon.

If the particular states in this country would prefer to stand in a similar relationship with each other, and to drop the project of a general government in favor of specific alliances, we would fall prey to all of the problems of instability and conflict just described. Such a relationship would, however, at least be consistent and practicable. Abandoning all thought of a confederate government, we would have simple offensive and defensive alliances. This would place us in the position of alternate friends and enemies of each other, as our different interests and competitions—encouraged by the influence of foreign nations—should incline us.

But if we prefer to have a national government rather than temporary and shifting alliances, our plan must have those ingredients which differentiate a government from an alliance. We must extend the authority of the Union to the persons of the citizens, who are the only proper objects of government.

Government implies the power of making laws. It is essential to the idea of a law that it include a penalty or punishment for disobedience. Without this, the commands which pretend to be laws will, in fact, amount to nothing more than advice or recommendation. Such penalties can only be applied in two ways: by courts and judges, or by military force—by judicial coercion or by military coercion. The first kind of coercion can only apply to men, while the second kind is the only one available against independent states. There is no judicial process by which the observance of the laws can, in the last resort, be enforced against states. Courts may rule against them for violations of their duty, but these rulings can only be enforced by military means. In an association where the general authority is limited to acting upon the states that compose it as political units, every violation of the laws must involve a state of war, and military force must become the only means of enforcing obedience. This state of things cannot deserve the name of "government," nor would any intelligent man choose to pursue his happiness within it.

There was a time when we were told that violations by the states of federal regulations were not to be expected, and that a sense of the common interest would inspire them to fully comply with all of the constitutional requisitions of the Union. This language now sounds unbelievable, as will the similar claims of the new Constitution's opponents once we have received further lessons from experience, which is the best oracle of wisdom. Such opinions show an ignorance of the true motivations of human actions and deny the very reason for establishing governments in the first place. Why has government been established at all? Because the passions of men will not be led by reason and justice unless they are constrained to do so by some external force.[2] Do groups of men tend to act with more reason and justice than individuals? The opposite seems to be the case from observation, and is supported by obvious reasons. When the responsibility for a bad action is divided among a number rather than falling directly upon one, each is likely to feel the restraint of embarrassment or shame less. And when a spirit of faction is mixed with the deliberations of a group, each person rushes to judgments and decisions which they would hesitate to make on their own.

In addition to all this, holding sovereign political power makes those who wield it naturally suspicious of all external attempts to control or restrain their power. As a result of this, in every political association which unites a number of smaller political units within a single larger one, there will be a natural tendency on the part of the smaller ones to escape the control and influence of the larger. This tendency is easy to account for. It has its origin in the love of power. Controlled or diminished power is almost always the enemy of the power which controls or diminishes it. This simple observation suggests that we should not expect state politicians to be always ready and eager to carry out the decrees of the national authority. The opposite of this results from the constitution of human nature.

If, therefore, national measures cannot be carried out without the intervention of the particular state governments, there will be little hope of their being carried out at all. State politicians will take it upon themselves to judge the propriety of the measures, whether or not they have a constitutional right to do so. They will consider how the proposed measure or requirement fits their immediate interests and goals, and the temporary conveniences or inconveniences that would accompany its adoption. All of this will be done without that knowledge of national circumstances and reasons of state which is essential to a correct judgment, and with that strong preference for local purposes which will always mislead the decision. The same process will be repeated in every state, and the carrying out of the plans constructed by the national Congress will always vary according to the ignorant and biased opinions of each state. It is very difficult to bring a single assembly of people to a harmonious agreement on important points. When there is a number of such assemblies, deliberating separately, at different times, and with different circumstances, such agreement becomes impossible.

In our case, the unanimous agreement of thirteen distinct sovereign political units is required, under the Articles of Confederation, for the carrying out of every important measure that comes from the Union. We might have known what the result of this would be. The measures of the Union have not been carried out, and the failures of the states to comply have become so extreme as to bring the wheels of the national government to a grinding halt. Congress can now barely keep up the ordinary administrative operations of the national government until the states agree on a more substantial substitute for our shadow of a federal government.

Things did not come to this desperate stage all at once. The causes which I have discussed produced, at first, only unequal and disproportionate degrees of compliance with the Union's measures. The greater irresponsibility of some states gave a bad example and increased temptation to those states which were initially more responsible. Why, they asked, should we bear a heavier share of the burden than other members of the Union? This was a question which human selfishness could not withstand, even among the more rational and prudent state leaders. Each state, giving in to the powerful voice of immediate interest or convenience, has one by one withdrawn its support of the Union. The frail and tottering building now seems ready to fall upon our heads and to crush us beneath its ruins.

Federalist 37

[Madison]

We have considered several of the most important principles of the proposed government, and have shown that the defects of the existing Confederation cannot be remedied by a government any less powerful than the one proposed. But because the ultimate goal of these papers is to determine clearly and fully the merits of this Constitution—and the desirability of actually adopting it—we must take a more thorough survey of the work of the Constitutional Convention. We must examine it from every angle, compare it in all its parts, and calculate its likely effects.

In order to pursue this examination in a just and fair-minded way, we must first reflect upon the difficulties that will tend to hinder many from being honest and straightforward in their assessment of the work of the convention.

The first difficulty is the common human failure to investigate public measures with that spirit of moderation which is essential to an accurate evaluation of their potential for advancing or injuring the public good. This spirit of moderation is, moreover, usually diminished as the importance of the measure under consideration increases.[1] It is not surprising, then, that the act of the convention—an act which recommends so many important changes and innovations, which may be looked at from so many different angles and perspectives, and which affects so many personal passions and interests—should find or give rise to dispositions that are unfriendly to a fair discussion and accurate judgment of its merits, on both sides of the debate. It is obvious that some have decided to condemn the proposed Constitution before even looking at it. Others have decided in advance to approve it. The opinions of both of these groups should, therefore, be given little consideration.

Although the opinions of both of these groups should be given little consideration, there may be some difference in the purity of their intentions. Those who have rushed to approve the work of the convention may have done so either because they are considering the critical nature of our situation and the necessity of doing something to relieve it, or because they have some sinister motive. Those who have rushed to disapprove of the work of the convention, on the other hand, cannot have been led by any honest and pardonable motive. The intentions of the first may be either upright or blamable. The views of the last cannot be upright, and must be blamable. But the truth is that these papers are not addressed to either of these groups. They are addressed only to those who combine a sincere zeal for the happiness of their country with the disposition to fairly judge the best means of promoting it.

Such persons will approach a reading of the plan proposed by the convention not only without a disposition to find or magnify faults, but also with the realization that they shouldn't expect a perfect plan. They will also consider not only the fact that the convention members, as human beings, were fallible in constructing the proposed Constitution, but also that they themselves are also fallible in their judgment of it.

Beyond these considerations relating to the persons involved, one must also make allowances for the difficulties involved in the nature of the convention's task itself.

The novelty of the task is immediately striking. We have shown in these papers that the existing Confederation is founded on incorrect principles, and that we must completely change this foundation along with the structure resting upon it. We have also shown that all previous confederacies in history have been founded on the same incorrect principles, and can therefore only be used as examples of what to avoid. The best that the convention could do, therefore, was to avoid the mistakes made both by these previous confederacies as well as our own, and then to provide a convenient process by which their own errors could be remedied in the future.

One of the most important difficulties encountered by the convention must have consisted in the question of how to combine the necessary stability and efficiency in government with the necessary attention due to liberty and to the republican form.[2] They needed to substantially address this difficulty in order to fulfill the goal of the convention and the expectations of the public, but anyone familiar with the subject will agree that doing so could not have been easy. Efficiency in government is essential to securing citizens against external and internal dangers, and to the effective execution of the laws which enters into the very definition of good government. Stability in government is essential to national character and to the advantages that attend it, as well as to the peace of mind and confidence of the people, which are among the most important blessings of civil society. An inconsistent and constantly changing legislation is both evil in itself and hateful to the people. These people, enlightened as they are about the nature of good government and interested as they are in its effects, will never be satisfied until some remedy is applied to the instability of the state administrations.

On comparing, however, these valuable ingredients of stability and efficiency with the vital principles of liberty, we see at once the difficulty involved in mixing them together in the proper proportions. The idea of republican liberty seems to demand, on the one hand, not only that all power should be derived from the people, but that those entrusted with this power should be kept responsible to the people by short terms. Even during these short terms, moreover, this trust should be placed in a larger rather than a smaller number of representatives. Stability, on the other hand, requires that political power should continue to be entrusted to the same people for a long period of time. Frequent elections will result in frequent changes of representatives, and frequent changes of representatives will result in frequent changes in legislation. And efficiency in government requires not only a certain duration of power, but the execution of it by a single hand.

How well the convention succeeded in addressing this difficulty will appear more clearly on a more accurate view of their work. From the brief view taken here, it clearly appears to have been a very difficult part of this work.

No less difficult must have been the task of determining the proper boundary between the authority of the general government and that of the state governments. Anyone who is familiar with contemplating and distinguishing between objects that are wide-ranging and complicated in their nature will appreciate this difficulty. The faculties of the mind itself have never yet been completely and persuasively distinguished and defined despite the efforts of the most brilliant philosophers. Sense, perception, judgment, desire, the will, memory, and imagination seem to be separated by such vague and small differences that their boundaries are still widely discussed and debated. The boundaries between the great kingdoms of nature, and, even more, between its various subdivisions, provide another example of the same important truth. The most brilliant and hardworking naturalists have never yet succeeded in tracing with certainty the line which separates plant life from the neighboring region of unorganized matter, or that which separates animal life from plants. Even more uncertainty lies in the distinctive features by which the beings in each of these great departments of nature have been arranged and assorted.

The works of nature are, though, perfectly defined in themselves, and only appear confusing to us because of our imperfection. In turning to human institutions, which are not so perfectly defined because they are the products of human construction, the uncertainty must be even greater. History teaches us that political science has not yet been able to define, with sufficient certainty, the three primary branches of government: the legislative, executive, and judiciary. Even the privileges and powers of the different legislative branches have yet to be so defined. Everyday experience raises questions which prove the shortcomings of political science and puzzle its best students.

Long experience, along with the combined efforts of the most enlightened legislators and lawyers, has been similarly unsuccessful in defining the objects and limits of different legal codes and different courts. The precise extent of the common law, statute law, maritime law, ecclesiastical law, corporate law, and other local laws and customs is still unclear even in Great Britain, where these subjects have been most thoroughly investigated. The jurisdictions of Britain's several courts is equally unclear. All new laws, though written with great skill and debated at length, are considered overly vague and general until their meaning is determined by a series of particular discussions and applications.

Besides the difficulties arising from the complexity of objects and the imperfection of our human powers of perception, the vehicle for communicating our ideas to one another adds another dimension of difficulty. The use of words is to express ideas. Clarity of expression, therefore, requires not only that the ideas be clearly formed, but also that they be expressed by words specifically and exclusively paired with them. But no language can supply words and phrases for every complex idea, and every language includes many words that contain multiple meanings. Therefore it happens that however accurately an object may be defined in itself, and however accurately this definition may be understood, the definition as expressed in language may still be rendered inaccurate by the inaccuracy of the words comprising it. And this unavoidable inaccuracy must be greater or less according to the complexity and novelty of the object being defined. When the Almighty Himself sees fit to address mankind in their own language, His meaning, clear as it must be in itself, is rendered dim and doubtful by the cloudy medium through which it is communicated.

There are, then, three sources of vague and incorrect definitions: (1) indistinctness of the object, (2) imperfection of our human powers of perception, and (3) shortcomings of the vehicle for communicating ideas. Any one of these must produce a certain amount of uncertainty. The Constitutional Convention, in defining the boundary between the federal and state jurisdictions, must have experienced the full effect of them all.

To the difficulties already mentioned may be added the contradictory aims of the larger and smaller states. The larger states would, of course, argue for a greater role in the new government on account of their superior wealth and importance; while the smaller states would argue for retaining the equality they presently enjoy under the existing Confederation. Because neither side could be expected to yield entirely to the other, this disagreement could only end in compromise. It is extremely probable, also, that after the ratio of representation had been adjusted, this very compromise must have given rise to a new struggle between the larger and smaller states over the powers and importance of the branches in which each had gained the greatest share of influence. There are features in the Constitution that reflect each of these struggles, which shows that the convention was forced, at times, to sacrifice pure logic to practical considerations.

Nor could the large and small states have been the only conflicting groups. Others arising from differences of location and customs must have created additional difficulties. Just as every state may be divided into different districts, and its citizens into different classes, which give rise to competing interests and local prejudices, so also the different parts of the United States are distinguished from each other by many circumstances which produce a similar effect on a larger scale. And although this variety of interests, as explained in *Federalist* 10, may have a good influence on the administration of the government when it is already formed, it must have had the opposite influence on the convention's task of forming it.

Would it then be hard to believe if, under the pressure of all these difficulties, the convention should have been forced into some deviations from the abstract ideal which a political theorist might plan in his closet?[3] The real wonder is that so many difficulties should have been overcome, and overcome with a unanimity as unprecedented as it must have been unexpected. It is impossible for any honest person to reflect on this fact without being amazed. It is impossible for any pious person not to see in it the same hand of the Almighty which so frequently came to our assistance in the critical stages of the Revolution.

We mentioned in a previous paper the repeated and unsuccessful attempts which have been made in the United Netherlands to reform the notorious defects of their constitution. The history of almost all the great assemblies held among mankind for resolving their disagreements, overcoming their prejudices, and accommodating their respective interests is a history of factions, struggles, and disappointments which may be ranked among the darkest and most degraded representations of the weaknesses and evils of human nature.[4] If we see a brighter representation of human nature in a few scattered cases, these serve only as the exceptions that prove the rule, and by their brightness to darken the gloom of our normal experience. In reviewing the causes from which these exceptions result, and applying them to the particular cases in front of us, we are necessarily led to two important conclusions. The first is that the convention must have enjoyed, to an extraordinary degree, a freedom from the harmful influence of party conflict—the disease most common to deliberative assemblies, and most likely to contaminate their proceedings. The second conclusion is that all of the delegations composing the convention were satisfied with the final product. Or, at least, they were led to endorse it by a deep conviction of the necessity of sacrificing their private opinions and partial interests to the public good, and by the unlikelihood that delays or alternative proposals would lessen this necessity.

Federalist 39

[Madison]

The last paper having concluded the observations which were meant to introduce a fair-minded consideration of the plan of government produced by the convention, we now proceed to examine that plan of government itself.

The first question we have to consider is whether the general form and features of the government are strictly republican. It is clear that no other form of government would be compatible with the character of the American people, with the fundamental principles of the Revolution, or with the noble goal of basing all our political experiments on the capability of mankind for self-government.[1] If, therefore, the plan of the convention departs from the republican form, its advocates must abandon it as no longer defensible.

What, then, are the distinctive features of the republican form? If we look for an answer to this question in the way political writers have applied the term to actual governments, instead of going back to principles, we won't ever find it. Holland is almost universally called a "republic," though no part of the ultimate political authority is derived from the people. The same title has been given to Venice, where a small group of hereditary nobles exercises absolute power over the people in the most absolute manner. Poland, which is a mixture of the worst forms of aristocracy and monarchy, has been honored with the same name. The government of England, which has only one republican branch combined with a hereditary aristocracy and monarchy, has also been often placed on the list of "republics." These examples, which are very different from each other as well as from a genuine republic, show the extreme inaccuracy with which the term has been used in political writings.

If, on the other hand, we go back to the different principles lying at the foundation of different forms of government, we may define a "republic" to be a government which (1) derives all its powers directly or indirectly from the people, and (2) is administered by persons holding their offices during pleasure, for a definite term, or during good behavior.[2] It is *essential* to a republic that it be derived from the people as a whole, rather than a small part or elite class of the people. Otherwise, a handful of tyrannical nobles might claim for their government the honorable title of "republic" by exercising their oppressions through a delegation of their powers to politicians. It is *sufficient* for such a government that the persons administering it be appointed, either directly or indirectly, by the people, and that they hold their appointments by one of the periods of time just mentioned. Otherwise, every government in the United States, as well as every other good and effective popular government, would be disqualified from being a republic. According to the constitution of every state in the Union, at least some government officials are appointed only indirectly by the people. According to most of them, the governor himself is so appointed. And according to one, this method of indirect appointment is adopted in one of the two branches of the legislature. According to all the constitutions, also, the governor has a definite term, and in many cases, both within the legislative and executive departments, this term extends to a period of years. According to most of the constitutions, again, as well as according to the best opinions on the subject, judges hold their offices during good behavior.

Comparing the Constitution planned by the convention with this standard, we can see immediately that it is strictly in agreement with it. The House of Representatives, like at least one branch of all the state legislatures, is elected directly by the people. The Senate, like the Congress in the existing Confederation, and the senate of Maryland, is appointed indirectly by the people. The President is elected indirectly by the people, following the example in most of the states. Even the judges and all the other officers of the Union will, as in the several states, be the choice, however indirect, of the people themselves.

The duration of the appointments is equally in agreement with the republican standard, and to the example of the state constitutions. The House of Representatives is elected periodically, as in all the states; and for the period of two years, as in the state of South Carolina. The Senate is elected for the period of six years, which is only one more year than that of the senate of Maryland, and only two more than that of the senates of New York and Virginia. The President has a term of four years; as in New York and Delaware the governor is elected for three years, and in South Carolina for two years. The other states have annual elections for governor. Several of the states, however, make no constitutional provision for the impeachment of the governor. And in Delaware and Virginia he is not impeachable until he has left office. The President of the United States, on the other hand, is impeachable at any time during his term in office. The judges hold their offices during good behavior, as it undoubtedly should be. The terms of the ministerial offices in general will be a subject of legal regulation, according to the particular case and the example of the state constitutions.

The most decisive proof of the republican nature of the proposed Constitution, though, might be found in its absolute prohibition of titles of nobility both in the federal and the state governments, as well as in its explicit guarantee of the republican form of government to each of the states.

"But it was not enough," say the opponents of the proposed Constitution, "for the convention to follow the republican form. They should have equally preserved the *federal* form, which views the Union as a *confederacy* of sovereign states. Instead, they have framed a *national* government, which views the Union as a *consolidation* of the states." And these opponents ask: "By what authority was this bold and radical change attempted?" The influence this objection has had requires that it should be examined very carefully.

Without questioning the accuracy of the distinction between a *confederacy* and a *consolidation* upon which the objection is based, in order to fairly evaluate the objection it will be necessary to accomplish three tasks: (1) to ascertain the real nature of the proposed government; (2) to investigate whether the convention was authorized to propose such a government; and (3) to determine how far the duty they owed to their country could make up for any lack of regular authority.

(1) In order to ascertain the real nature of the government, this government may be viewed according to five relations: (a) to the foundation on which it is to be established; (b) to the sources from which its ordinary powers are to be derived; (c) to the operation of those powers; (d) to the extent of them; and (e) to the authority for making amendments.

On examining the first relation (a), it seems, on the one hand, that the Constitution is to be founded on the consent of the American people, given by representatives elected for the special purpose. On the other hand, though, this consent is to be given by the people as individuals forming the distinct and independent states of which they are citizens, rather than as forming one entire nation. It is to be the consent of the states, derived from the ultimate authority in each state—the authority of the people themselves. The act, therefore, of establishing the Constitution will be a *federal* rather than a *national* act.

That it will be a federal and not a national act, as these terms are understood by the objectors—the act of the people as forming the several states rather than as forming one nation—is obvious from the fact that it is to result neither from the decision of a *majority* of the people of the Union, nor from that of a *majority* of the states. It must result from the *unanimous* consent of the several states that are parties to it, differing only from their ordinary consent in the fact that it is expressed by the people themselves rather than the legislature. If the people were treated in the ratification process as forming one nation, the majority would bind the minority just as the majority within each state binds the minority. And this majority must be determined either through individual votes, or by considering the will of the majority of the states as evidence of the will of a majority of the people of the United States. Neither of these rules has been adopted. In ratifying the Constitution, each state is viewed as a sovereign and independent entity, and is only to be bound by its own will. In this relation (a), then, the new Constitution will, if established, be a *federal* rather than a *national* one.

The next relation is to the sources (b) from which the ordinary powers of government are to be derived. The House of Representatives will derive its powers from the American people, and the people will be represented in the same way as they are in the legislature of a particular state. In this way the government is *national*, not *federal*. The Senate, on the other hand, will derive its powers from the states as sovereign and independent entities; and these will be represented equally in the Senate as they now are in the Congress of the existing Confederation. In this way the government is *federal*, not *national*. The executive power will be derived from a very compound source. The immediate election of the President is to be made by the states as sovereign and independent entities. The votes are distributed to them in a compound ratio which views them partly as equal societies and partly as unequal members of the same society. The eventual election, again, is to be made by the branch of the legislature which consists of the national representatives of the American people. In this particular act, though, they are to be viewed as delegations from several equal and independent states. From this relation, the government seems to have a mixed character, possessing both *federal* and *national* features.

The difference between a *federal* and a *national* government as it relates to its *operation* (c) consists in this: in a *federal* government, the powers operate on the states forming the Confederacy as sovereign and independent entities; in a *national* government, these powers operate on the individual citizens forming the nation. Viewing the Constitution according to this relation, it is *national*, and not *federal*; though perhaps not as completely as some might think. In several cases, and particularly in legal controversies in which states may be parties, they must be viewed as collective entities only. In this way the national face of the government seems to be disfigured by a few federal features. But this blemish is perhaps unavoidable in any plan; and the operation of the government on the people as individual citizens in its ordinary and most essential activities may, on the whole, designate it a *national* government.

But if the government is national with respect to the *operation* of its powers, it changes again when we view it in relation to the extent of its powers (d). The idea of a national government implies not only an authority over individual citizens, but a general supremacy over all persons and things so far as they are objects of lawful government. Among a people consolidated into one nation, this supremacy is completely located in the national legislature. Among peoples united for particular purposes, it is located partly in the national and partly in the state legislatures. In the first case, all state governments are subordinated to the national one, and may be controlled, directed, or abolished by it whenever it likes. In the second case, the state governments form distinct and independent parts of the supremacy, no more subordinate to the national authority, within their respective spheres, than the national authority is subordinate to them within its own sphere. In this relation, then, the proposed government cannot be called a *national* one, since its jurisdiction extends to certain enumerated objects only, and leaves to the states a residual and inviolable sovereignty over all other objects.

It is true that in controversies relating to the borders between two jurisdictions, the authority which is ultimately to decide is to be a national one. But this does not change the principle of the case. The decision is to be impartially made according to the rules of the Constitution; and all the usual and most effective precautions are taken to ensure this impartiality. Such a final authority is clearly necessary to prevent warfare and a dissolving of the constitutional compact. And it is obvious that this final authority should be established under the national rather than the state governments.

If we view the Constitution by its last relation to the authority for making amendments (e), we find it neither entirely *national* nor entirely *federal*. If it were entirely national, the supreme and ultimate authority would rest with the *majority* of the people of the Union. This authority would be able at any time, like that of a majority of every national society, to alter or abolish its established government. If it were entirely federal, on the other hand, the agreement of each state in the Union would be necessary for every change that would be binding on all of them. The method provided by the plan of the convention does not follow either of these principles. By requiring more than a majority, and by calculating the proportion by *states* rather than by *citizens*, it is more *federal* than *national*. By making the agreement of less than the total number of states sufficient, on the other hand, it is more *national* than *federal*.

The proposed Constitution, therefore, is, in fact, neither a national nor a federal Constitution, but a combination of both.[3] In its foundation it is federal, not national. In the sources from which the ordinary powers of the government are derived, it is partly federal and partly national. In the operation of these powers, it is national, not federal. In the extent of them, it is federal, not national. And, finally, in the authority for making amendments, it is neither entirely federal nor entirely national.

Federalist 47

[Madison]

Having reviewed the general form of the proposed government and the general mass of power given to it, I proceed to examine the particular structure of this government, as well as the distribution of this mass of power among its particular parts.

One of the main objections raised by the more respectable opponents of the Constitution is its supposed violation of the political principle that the legislative, executive, and judiciary departments should be separate and distinct. They say that no regard seems to have been paid to this essential safeguard of liberty in the structure of the federal government. The different departments of power are distributed and blended in such a manner as to destroy all balance and beauty of form, and to expose some of the essential parts of the structure to the danger of being crushed by the excessive weight of other parts.

No political truth is of greater intrinsic value, or is endorsed by more enlightened friends of liberty, than that on which the objection is founded. The accumulation of all powers, legislative, executive, and judiciary, in the same hands—whether of one, a few, or many, and whether hereditary, self-appointed, or elected—may fairly be called the very definition of tyranny.[1] If the federal Constitution were really guilty of this charge of accumulation of powers, or of a mixture of powers tending to such accumulation, no further arguments would be necessary to inspire a universal rejection of it. I am convinced, though, that the charge cannot be supported, and that the principle on which it is founded has been totally misunderstood and misapplied. In order to form correct ideas on this important subject, we must investigate the particular sense in which the preservation of liberty requires that the three departments of power should be separate and distinct.

The authority who is always cited on this subject is the celebrated Montesquieu. If he is not the author of this invaluable political principle, he has at least presented and recommended it most effectively to the attention of mankind. Let us attempt, first, to ascertain his meaning on this point.

The British Constitution was to Montesquieu what Homer has been to scholars of epic poetry. As scholars have considered Homer's work as the perfect model from which the principles and rules of the art were to be drawn, and by which all similar works were to be judged, so Montesquieu appears to have viewed the British Constitution as the standard or "mirror" of political liberty; and to have shown, in the form of basic truths, the several characteristic principles of that particular system. So that we may be sure not to misunderstand his meaning, let us return to the source from which the principle was drawn.

On the most casual view of the British Constitution, we see that the legislative, executive, and judiciary departments are by no means totally separate and distinct from each other. The executive magistrate forms an integral part of the legislative authority. He alone has the prerogative of making treaties with foreign nations, which have the force of legislative acts. All the members of the judiciary department are appointed by him, can be removed by him when called for by the two Houses of Parliament, and form one of his constitutional councils. One branch of the legislative department forms also a great constitutional council to the executive magistrate, while at the same time being the sole depository of judicial power in cases of impeachment, and is invested with the supreme appellate jurisdiction in all other cases. The judges, too, are so far connected with the legislative department as often to attend and participate in its deliberations, although not allowed to vote.

From these facts, by which Montesquieu was guided, it may clearly be inferred that when he said "There can be no liberty where the legislative and executive powers are united in the same person, or body of magistrates," or "if the power of judging be not separated from the legislative and executive powers . . .," he did not mean that these departments ought to have no *partial role* in, or no *control* over, the acts of each other. His meaning, according to his own words, and even more convincingly illustrated by the British Constitution, can amount only to this: where the *whole* power of one department is exercised by the same hands which exercise the *whole* power of another, the fundamental principles of a free constitution are violated.

This would have been the case in the British Constitution if the king, who is the executive magistrate, had possessed also the whole legislative power, or the whole administration of justice; or if the legislature had possessed the whole judiciary power, or the whole executive power. This, however, is not among the faults of that constitution. The king cannot himself make a law, though he can veto every law. Nor can he administer justice in person, though he can appoint those who do administer it. The judges cannot exercise executive prerogative, though they are appointed by the executive. Nor can they exercise any legislative function, though they may attend and participate in the legislative councils. The legislature cannot perform any judiciary act, though it may remove judges from their offices by the joint act of two of its branches, and though one of its branches possesses the judicial power in the last resort. Nor can the legislature exercise executive prerogative, though one of its branches constitutes the supreme executive magistracy, and another can try and condemn all the subordinate officers in the executive department in cases of impeachment.

The reasons on which Montesquieu grounds his principle are a further demonstration of his meaning. "When the legislative and executive powers are united in the same person or body," he says, "there can be no liberty, because apprehensions may arise lest *the same* monarch or senate should *enact* tyrannical laws to *execute* them in a tyrannical manner." Again: "Were the power of judging joined with the legislative, the life and liberty of the subject would be exposed to arbitrary control, for *the judge* would then be *the legislator*. Were it joined to the executive power, *the judge* might behave with all the violence of *an oppressor*." These passages sufficiently establish the meaning which we have put on this celebrated principle of this celebrated author.

If we look into the constitutions of the states, we find that there is not a single instance in which the different departments of power have been kept absolutely separate and distinct, despite the emphatic and clear terms in which this principle has been laid down. New Hampshire, whose constitution was the last formed, seems to have been fully aware of the impossibility and imprudence of avoiding any mixture whatsoever of these powers, and has modified the doctrine by declaring "that the legislative, executive, and judiciary powers ought to be kept as separate from, and independent of, each other *as the nature of a free government will admit; or as is consistent with that chain of connection that binds the whole fabric of the constitution in one indissoluble bond of unity and amity.*" Her constitution accordingly mixes these powers in several ways. The Senate, which is a branch of the legislative department, is also a judicial tribunal for the trial of impeachments. The president, who is the head of the executive department, is also the presiding member of the Senate, having both an equal vote in all cases and a casting vote in case of a tie. The executive head is himself eventually elected every year by the legislative department, and his council is chosen by and from the legislative department every year. Several of the officers of state are also appointed by the legislature. And the members of the judiciary department are appointed by the executive department.

The constitution of Massachusetts has followed a similar path in expressing this fundamental principle of liberty. It declares "that the legislative departments shall never exercise the executive and judicial powers, or either of them; the executive shall never exercise the legislative and judicial powers, or either of them; the judicial shall never exercise the legislative and executive powers, or either of them." This declaration corresponds precisely with Montesquieu's doctrine, as it has been explained, and is not in a single point violated by the plan of the convention. It goes no farther than to prohibit any one of the entire departments from exercising the powers of another department. In the very constitution to which it is prefixed, a partial mixture of powers has been admitted. The executive magistrate has a qualified veto on the legislature, and the Senate, which is a part of the legislature, is a court of impeachment for members both of the executive and judiciary departments. The members of the judiciary department are appointed by the executive department and removable by the same authority on the petition of the two legislative branches. Lastly, a number of the officers of government are annually appointed by the legislative department. Because the appointment to executive offices is in its nature an executive function, the designers of this constitution have, in this last point at least, violated the rule they themselves established.

I will not examine the constitutions of Rhode Island and Connecticut, because they were formed prior to the Revolution and even before the political principle we are discussing had become commonly accepted.

The constitution of New York does not contain any declaration on this subject, but it seems very clearly to have been framed with a view to the danger of improperly blending the different departments of government. Nevertheless, it gives to both the executive magistrate and the judiciary department a partial control over the legislature, even blending the executive and judiciary departments in the exercise of this control. Members of the legislature are associated with the executive authority in its council of appointment, appointing both executive and judiciary officers. And its court for impeachment trials and correction of errors consists of one branch of the legislature and the principal members of the judiciary department.

The constitution of New Jersey has blended the different powers of government more than any of the preceding ones. The governor, who is the executive magistrate, is appointed by the legislature. He is chancellor and ordinary, or surrogate of the state. He is a member of the Supreme Court of Appeals, and president, with a casting vote, of one of the legislative branches. The same legislative branch acts as the governor's executive council, and joins him in constituting the Court of Appeals. The members of the judiciary department are appointed by the legislature, and removable by one branch of it upon the impeachment of the other.

According to the constitution of Pennsylvania, the president, who is the executive magistrate, is annually elected by a vote in which the legislative department predominates. Together with an executive council, he appoints the members of the judiciary department and forms a court of impeachment for trial of all officers, judiciary as well as executive. The judges of the Supreme Court and justices of the peace seem also to be removable by the legislature. The executive power of pardoning is also, in certain cases, to be referred to the legislature. The members of the executive council are, finally, made ex-officio justices of peace throughout the state.

In Delaware, the chief executive magistrate is annually elected by the legislature. The speakers of the two legislative branches are vice presidents in the executive department. The executive chief, together with six others appointed by the legislative branches (three by each), constitute the Supreme Court of Appeals. The executive chief is joined with the legislature in the appointment of the other judges. Throughout the states, it seems that the members of the legislature may at the same time be justices of the peace. In this state, the members of one branch of the legislature are ex-officio justices of the peace, as are the members of the executive council. The main officers of the executive department are appointed by the legislature, and one branch of the legislature forms a court of impeachments. All officers may be removed on petition of the legislature.

Maryland has adopted the political principle we are discussing in the strongest terms, declaring that the legislative, executive, and judicial powers of government ought to be forever separate and distinct from each other. Nevertheless, her constitution makes the executive magistrate appointable by the legislature, and the members of the judiciary by the executive department.

The language of Virginia is even stronger on this subject. Her constitution declares "that the legislative, executive, and judiciary departments shall be separate and distinct; so that neither exercise the powers properly belonging to the other; nor shall any person exercise the powers of more than one of them at the same time, except that the justices of county courts shall be eligible to either House of Assembly." Despite this strong declaration, we find other exceptions in addition to the explicit one mentioned. The chief executive magistrate, with his executive council, are appointable by the legislature. Two members of the executive council are removed every three years by the legislature. And all the main offices, both executive and judiciary, are filled by the legislature as well. The executive power of pardoning, also, is in one case placed in the legislature.

The constitution of North Carolina, which declares "that the legislative, executive, and supreme judicial powers of government ought to be forever separate and distinct from each other," nevertheless gives the legislature the power of appointing not only the chief executive magistrate but all of the main officers within both the executive and judiciary department.

In South Carolina, the constitution gives the legislative department the power of electing the executive magistrate. It gives to the legislature, also, the power of appointing the members of the judiciary department, including even justices of the peace and sheriffs. It also gives to the legislature the power of appointing officers in the executive department, down to captains in the army and navy of the state.

In the constitution of Georgia, where it is declared "that the legislative, executive, and judiciary departments shall be separate and distinct, so that neither exercise the powers properly belonging to the other," we find that the executive department is to be filled by appointments of the legislature. The legislature is also given the authority of exercising the executive power of pardoning, and even justices of the peace are to be appointed by the legislature.

I do not describe these cases in which the three departments have not been kept totally separate and distinct in order to argue for the particular way in which the various state governments have organized them. I am fully aware that, although the state constitutions reflect many excellent principles, they also reflect the haste and inexperience under which they were designed. It is obvious that in some cases the fundamental principle we are discussing has been violated by an excessive mixture, and even consolidation, of the three different powers. In no case, moreover, has a sufficient provision been made for enforcing in practice the separation laid out on paper. My point has been to defend the proposed Constitution against the charge of violating this sacred principle of free government. This charge is warranted neither by the real meaning given to that principle by Montesquieu, nor by the sense in which our state constitutions have understood it. This interesting subject will be continued in the next paper.

Federalist 49

[Madison]

The author of the "Notes on the State of Virginia" (Thomas Jefferson) has added to that valuable work the draft of a constitution for Virginia, to be laid before a convention called by the state legislature in 1783. The plan, like everything else written by this author, shows an original, comprehensive, and accurate way of thinking. It is particularly worthy of our attention because it shows both a fervent attachment to republican government and an enlightened view of the dangerous tendencies against which such a government ought to be guarded. One of the guards which he proposes, and on which he seems ultimately to rely as a reinforcement for the weaker departments of power against the domination of the stronger, is perhaps entirely original. Because it directly relates to the subject currently under discussion, we shouldn't overlook it.

His idea is "that whenever any two of the three branches of government shall concur in opinion, each by the voices of two-thirds of their whole number, that a convention is necessary for altering the constitution, or *correcting breaches of it*, a convention shall be called for the purpose."

Because the people are the only legitimate source of political power, and it is from them that the constitutional charter giving the branches of government their power is derived, it seems that republican theory would dictate returning to the same original authority not only whenever it may be necessary to alter the powers of government, but also whenever any one of the departments trespasses on the authorities of the others. Because each of the departments derive equally from this common authority, none of them can claim an exclusive or superior right of determining the boundaries between their respective powers. How, then, could the stronger departments be prevented from dominating the weaker without an appeal to the people themselves, who are alone capable of declaring the meaning of the constitution and enforcing its observance by those in government?

There is certainly great force in this reasoning, and it definitely indicates that a constitutional road to the decision of the people should be marked out and kept open for extraordinary occasions. But there seem to be decisive objections against the proposed appeal to the people as an ordinary way of keeping the three departments of power within their constitutional limits.

In the first place, the provision does not apply to the case of a combination of two of the departments against the third. If the legislative authority, which possesses so many means of influencing the other departments, were able to gain to its interest either of the others, or even one-third of its members, the remaining department would not be able to call a special convention. I will not dwell on this objection, though, because it might be thought to apply only to this particular part of the proposal rather than its underlying principle.

Turning to this underlying principle, it may be objected that, because every appeal to the people would imply some defect in the government, frequent appeals would largely deprive the government of that veneration upon which all governments, even the wisest and freest, depend for their stability.[1] If it is true that all governments rest on opinion, it is also true that the strength of each individual's opinion, and its practical influence on his behavior, depends much on the number of people whom he thinks have the same opinion. The reason of man, like man himself, is timid and cautious when it is alone, and acquires firmness and confidence in proportion to the number with which it is associated. When the examples that strengthen opinion are *ancient* in addition to being *numerous*, they are known to have a double effect on this firmness and confidence. In a nation of philosophers, of course, this consideration would not apply. Their enlightened reason would inspire a sufficient respect for the laws and constitution. But a nation of philosophers is as impossible as the philosopher-kings in Plato's *Republic*. And in every other nation, the most rational government will find it a powerful advantage to have the prejudices of the community on its side.

An even more serious objection against frequently appealing to the people for the decision of constitutional questions lies in the danger of disturbing the peace by enflaming the public passions. Although we have had success in revising our established forms of government, which speaks to the virtue and intelligence of the American people, doing so is always risky and shouldn't be attempted unnecessarily. We should remember that all the existing constitutions were formed in the midst of a danger which held down the passions opposed to order and agreement. They were formed during a time of an enthusiastic confidence of the people in their patriotic leaders, which limited the ordinary diversity of opinions on important national issues. There was a universal desire for new and different forms of government, brought on by a universal resentment and disapproval of the old one. And there was no spirit of partisanship to disrupt the effects of these positive influences; influences which, in future situations, we should not expect to usually enjoy.

But the greatest objection of all is that the decisions which would probably result from such appeals to the people would not serve the purpose of maintaining the constitutional balance of powers in the government. We have seen that republican governments tend to give disproportionate power to the legislative at the expense of the other two departments. The appeals to the people, therefore, would usually be made by the executive and judiciary departments. But whether they are made by one side or the other, would such appeals be expected to treat both sides fairly? Let us view the different situations of each side.

The members of the executive and judiciary departments are few in number, and only a small part of the people will know them personally. The members of the judiciary, because of their mode of appointment as well as the nature and permanency of it, are too far removed from the people to share much in their predispositions. The members of the executive are usually viewed with suspicion, and their administration is always liable to be tainted and rendered unpopular. The members of the legislative department, on the other hand, are numerous. They are distributed throughout and dwell among the people at large. Their connections of blood, of friendship, and of acquaintance include many of the most influential people in society. The nature of their public trust implies a personal influence among the people, and they seem to be more immediately the guardians of the rights and liberties of the people. As a result of these considerations, the legislative department would be expected to possess an unfair advantage in any appeal to the people.

But the legislative department would not only be able to plead their case most successfully with the people. They would probably be the judges themselves. The same influence which had secured their election to the legislature would also secure them a seat in the convention. Even if this wouldn't be the case with all the members of the legislature, it would probably be the case with many, and especially with the most influential ones who would be positioned to lead the convention. The convention would, then, be made up mostly of men who had been, who actually were, or who expected to be members of the same department whose conduct was on trial. They would be defendants and judges in the same case.

Sometimes, however, appeals might be made under circumstances more likely to be fair to the executive and judiciary departments. The violations of the legislature might be so obvious and sudden as to prevent attempts to portray them otherwise. A substantial part of the legislature might take side with the other branches. The President might be extremely popular. In such situations, the public decision might be less swayed by predispositions in favor of the legislature. Still, though, the decision on the appeal could never be expected to turn on the true merits of the question. It would inevitably be connected with the spirit of preexisting parties, or of interest groups springing out of the question itself. It would be connected with prominent people in society. It would be judged by the same men who had been proponents or opponents of the very measures whose constitutionality is being challenged. The *passions*, therefore, not the *reason*, of the public would sit in judgment. But it is the reason of the public that ought to control and regulate the government. The passions ought to be controlled and regulated by the government.[2]

We found in the last paper that mere written limitations are not enough to restrain the departments within their constitutional rights. From the discussion in this paper it appears that occasional appeals to the people would not be an appropriate or effective tool for that purpose either. I do not examine whether any other provisions of this author's plan might be adequate for the purpose. Some of them are unquestionably founded upon sound political principles, and all of them are crafted with exceptional innovation and precision.

Federalist 51

[Madison]

How, then, can we maintain in practice the necessary separation of powers laid down on paper in the Constitution? Because all external provisions have been found to be inadequate, the internal structure of the government must be designed in such a way that its individual parts may, through their interactions with one another, be the means of keeping each other in their proper places. Without attempting to provide a full explanation of this important idea, I will give a few general observations which may enable us to more correctly judge the principles and structure of the government planned by the convention.

In order to lay a good foundation for the separate and distinct exercise of the different powers of government—which all admit to be essential to the preservation of liberty—it is clear that each department of government should have a will of its own. It would seem, then, that the members of each department should have as little influence as possible in the appointment of the members of the others. If this principle were strictly followed, it would require that all the appointments for the supreme executive, legislative, and judiciary offices should be derived from the same source of authority, the people, through completely separate channels.

Perhaps such a plan of designing the several departments would be less difficult in practice than it seems in theory. Some difficulties, though, and some additional expense would be associated with this, and therefore some departures from the principle must be allowed. In the design of the judiciary department in particular, it might be imprudent to strictly insist on the principle. First, because special qualifications are essential in the members of the judiciary, the primary consideration ought to be to adopt that mode of appointment which best secures these qualifications. And secondly, because the permanent nature of their appointment would soon eliminate any feeling of dependence on the authority which appointed them.

It is equally clear that the members of each department should be as independent as possible from the others in the determination of their salary and benefits. If the executive magistrate, or the judges, were not independent of the legislature in this, their independence in every other way would be compromised.

But the great safeguard against a gradual concentration of the several powers in the same department consists in this: giving to the members of each department the necessary constitutional means and personal motives to resist encroachments by the others. The plan for defense must correspond to the danger of attack. Ambition must be made to counteract ambition. The interest of the man must be connected with the constitutional rights of his position. It may be a reflection on human nature that such a method is necessary to control the abuses of government. But what is government itself, but the greatest of all reflections on human nature? If men were angels, no government would be necessary. If angels governed men, neither external nor internal controls on government would be necessary. In designing a government by men and over men, the great difficulty is this: you must first enable the government to control the governed, and then you must force it to control itself.[1] The primary control on government is a dependence on the people; but experience has taught mankind the necessity of additional precautions.

This method of relying on opposing interests in the absence of better motives might be traced through all human affairs, private as well as public. We see it particularly displayed in all the subordinate distributions of power, where the constant goal is to divide and arrange offices in such a way that each may be a check on the other. The private self-interest of every individual may, in this way, be made a guardian of public rights. These inventions of prudence cannot be less necessary in the distribution of the supreme powers of the state.

But it is not possible to give each department an equal power of self-defense. In republican governments, the legislative department is necessarily the most powerful one. The solution for this is to divide the legislature into two branches, and to make them as little connected with each other as possible through different modes of election and different principles of action. It may even be necessary to implement more guards against dangerous encroachments. Just as the power of the legislative department requires that it should be divided, the weakness of the executive may require that its powers should be enlarged. An absolute veto on the legislature appears to be the natural defense with which the executive should be armed. But perhaps this wouldn't be completely safe nor sufficient by itself. On ordinary occasions it might not be used enough, and on extraordinary occasions it might be abused. Couldn't the veto power be supplemented by some connection between this weaker department and the weaker branch of the legislative department, by which the weaker branch of the legislative may be led to support the constitutional rights of the executive without being too detached from the rights of its own department?

If the principles on which these observations are founded are correct, as I believe they are, and if they are tested against both the several state constitutions and the federal Constitution, it will be found that the federal Constitution corresponds much more closely with them.

There are, moreover, two considerations particularly relevant to the federal system of America, which place that system in a very interesting light.

First: In a single republic, all the power given by the people resides in a single government, and abuses are guarded against by a division of the government into distinct and separate departments. In the compound republic of America, the power given by the people is first divided between two distinct governments, and then the portion given to each is subdivided among distinct and separate departments. Therefore the people have a double security for their rights.[2] The different governments will control each other, and at the same time each will be controlled by itself.

Second: In a republic it is very important not only to guard the people against the oppression of the government, but to guard one part of the people against oppression by the other part. Different interests necessarily exist in different classes of citizens. If a majority is united by a common interest, the rights of the minority will be insecure. There are only two methods of defending against this evil. One is by creating a will in the community independent of the majority—that is, independent of the people themselves. The other is by including within the people so many different types of citizens as to make an oppressive majority group very improbable, if not impossible.

The first method is adopted by all governments possessing a hereditary or self-appointed authority. This is, at best, a fragile security, because an authority independent of the people might just as well support the oppressive majority as the rightful minority, and such an authority might also be turned against both groups. The second method, on the other hand, will be adopted in the federal republic of the United States. While all authority in it will be derived from and dependent on the people, this people itself will be broken into so many parts, interests, and classes of citizens, that the rights of individuals, or of the minority, will be in little danger from an oppressive majority.

In a free government, the security for civil rights must be the same as that for religious rights. The first lies in a multitude of interests, and the second in a multitude of sects. The degree of security in both cases depends on the number of interests and sects, and this depends in turn on the size of the country and the number of people within it.

This treatment of the subject clearly shows the particular advantages of a proper federal system for successful republican government. It shows that oppressive majority groups will be more likely to form within separate and independent confederacies, or individual states, than throughout the territory of the Union. The best method for securing the rights of every class of citizen—the republican method of multiplying interests—would be diminished in effectiveness, leaving only the non-republican one of creating a will in the community independent of the people.

Justice is the goal of government. It is the goal of civil society. It always has been and always will be pursued until it is obtained, or until liberty is lost in the pursuit.[3] In a society within which the stronger faction can easily unite and oppress the weaker, anarchy reigns just as it does in a state of nature, where the weaker individual is subject to the violence of the stronger. And just as, in a state of nature, even the stronger individuals are led by the insecurity of their condition to submit to a government which protects all individuals, so, in an anarchic society, will the more powerful factions or parties gradually be led by the insecurity of their condition to wish for a government which protects all parties. If the state of Rhode Island were separated from the Confederacy and left to itself, the oppressions of majority factions would so frequently show the insecurity of rights under a popular form of government contained within a small area that these factions themselves would soon call for some power altogether independent of the people to protect their rights.

In the extended republic of the United States, and with the great variety of interests, parties, and sects which it includes, a coalition of a majority of the whole society could rarely take place on any other principles than those of justice and the general good.[4] And if there is less danger to a minority from the will of a majority, there must also be less reason to provide for the security of the minority by introducing into the government a will independent of the people. It is both certain and important, despite the disagreements of some, that the larger the society, as long as it remains within a practical sphere, the more capable it will be of self-government. And happily for the *republican cause*, this practical sphere can be extended very far by a careful modification and mixture of the *federal principle*.

Federalist 54

[Madison]

The next topic which I will treat regarding the House of Representatives relates to the determination of the number of representatives apportioned to each state, which is to be calculated by the same rule with that of direct taxes.

Everyone agrees that the number of people in each state should be the standard for regulating the proportion of those who are to represent the people of the state. The establishment of the same rule for the apportionment of taxes is similarly agreed upon, although the rule itself isn't founded on the same principle in both cases. In the case of representation, the rule refers to the personal rights of the people, with which it has a natural and universal connection. In the case of taxation, the rule refers to the proportion of wealth, of which population is never a precise measure, and even in ordinary cases a very inaccurate one. Despite the rule's imperfection as applied to the relative wealth and contributions of the states, it is clearly the most acceptable among the practicable rules, and had so recently obtained the general sanction of America that it was readily preferred also by the convention.

One might admit all this and still raise the following question: Does it follow, from an admission that numbers are an appropriate measure of representation, and that slaves combined with free citizens is an appropriate measure of wealth for purposes of taxation, that slaves ought to be included in the numerical rule of representation as well? Slaves are, after all, considered as property, not as persons. They ought therefore to be included in estimates of taxation which are founded on property, but excluded from representation which is determined by the number of persons. This is the objection, as I understand it, stated in its full force. I will be equally forceful in stating the argument which may be given on the opposing side.

"We agree with the idea," one of our southern brethren might observe, "that representation relates more directly to persons, and taxation more directly to property, and we agree that this idea should be applied to the case of our slaves. But we deny that slaves are considered merely as property, and in no respect at all as persons. The true fact of the matter is that they combine both these qualities: being considered by our laws, in some respects, as persons, and in other respects as property. In being forced to labor for a master rather than himself, in being sellable by one master to another master, and in being subject at all times to be restrained in his liberty and beaten in his body by the arbitrary will of another, the slave appears to be degraded from the human rank and grouped with those irrational animals which the law treats as property. On the other hand, in being protected in his life and limbs against the violence of all others (even the master of his labor and his liberty), and in being punishable himself for all violence committed against others, the slave is just as clearly treated by the law as a member of the society, and not as an irrational animal—as a moral person, and not as a mere piece of property.

"The federal Constitution, therefore, appropriately handles the case of our slaves when it views them as a mixture of persons and of property. This is in fact their true nature.[1] It is the nature given to them by the laws under which they live. And it can't be denied that the laws have this power, because it is only under the pretext that the laws have transformed the blacks into property that one might argue that they shouldn't be counted in the number of persons. And it is admitted that if the laws were to restore to them the rights which have been taken away, the blacks could no longer be refused an equal share of representation with the other inhabitants.

"This question can be looked at another way. Everyone agrees that numbers are the best measure of wealth and taxation as well as of representation. Would the convention have been unbiased or consistent if they had removed the slaves from the numbers in calculating representation, and added them to the numbers in calculating taxation? Could the southern states be reasonably expected to join a Union which considered their slaves as persons when burdens were to be imposed, but as property when benefits were to be distributed? And isn't it surprising that those who condemn the southern states for considering part of their human brethren as property, should themselves argue that the federal government ought to consider this unfortunate race more completely in the unnatural light of property than the very laws of which they complain?

"It may be replied, perhaps, that slaves are not included in the estimate of representatives in any of the states possessing them. They neither vote themselves nor increase the votes of their masters. Upon what principle, then, ought they to be taken into the federal estimate of representation? In rejecting them altogether, the Constitution would, in this respect, have followed the very laws which we have appealed to as the proper guide.

"This objection is refuted by a single observation. It is a fundamental principle of the proposed Constitution that, although the total number of representatives apportioned to the several states is to be determined by a federal rule based on the total number of inhabitants, the several states retain the power to designate which of their inhabitants possess the right of electing these representatives. The qualifications for voting rights are not, perhaps, the same in any two states. In some of the states the difference is very significant. In every state, a certain number of inhabitants are deprived of voting rights by the constitution of the state, who will nevertheless be included in the number of inhabitants according to which the federal Constitution apportions the representatives.

"In light of this, the southern states might object on their part that the principle laid down by the convention required that the policies of particular states toward their own inhabitants should not be considered at all. And if this is the case, the slaves, as inhabitants, should have been counted according to their full number, just like other inhabitants of states who do not enjoy any political rights. A strict adherence to this principle is, however, waived by the Southerners who would stand to gain by it. All that they ask is that equal moderation be shown on the other side. Let the case of the slaves be considered, as it really is, a peculiar one. Let the compromise of the Constitution be mutually adopted, which treats them as inhabitants, but as debased by servitude below the equal level of free inhabitants—which treats the *slave* as being deprived of two-fifths of the *man*.[2]

"After all, couldn't an additional argument be given in defense of this article of the Constitution? We have so far proceeded on the idea that representation should relate to persons only, and not at all to property. But is this idea correct? Government is instituted no less for the protection of the property, than of the persons, of individuals. The one as well as the other, therefore, may be considered as represented by those who are charged with the government. It is upon this principle that, in several of the states, and particularly in the state of New York, one branch of the government is intended especially to be the guardian of property, and is accordingly elected by the wealthier citizens. In the federal Constitution, this policy is not adopted. The rights of property are trusted in the same hands as personal rights. Some attention should, therefore, be given to property in the choice of those hands.

"For another reason, as well, the votes allowed in the federal legislature to the people of each state should bear some proportion to the comparative wealth of the states. States, unlike individuals, do not have an influence over each other arising from their comparative wealth. Although the law gives a wealthy citizen only a single vote in the election of his representative, the respect and influence which he derives from his wealth very often guides the votes of others to his choice. Through this informal channel, the rights of property are reflected in the public representation. A state possesses no such influence over other states. The richest state in the Confederacy will probably never influence the choice of a single representative in any other state. Nor will the representatives of the larger and richer states possess any other advantage in the federal legislature than what may result from their superior number alone. As far, therefore, as their superior wealth and weight might justly entitle them to any advantage, it should be given to them by a superior share of representation.

"The new Constitution is, in this respect, significantly different from the existing Confederation, as well as from that of the United Netherlands and other similar confederacies. In each of these others, the effectiveness of the federal resolutions depends on the subsequent and voluntary resolutions of the states composing the Union. Therefore the states, though they have an equal vote in the federal legislature, have an unequal influence corresponding with the unequal importance of these subsequent and voluntary resolutions. Under the proposed Constitution, federal laws will take effect without the necessary intervention of the individual states. They will depend merely on the majority of votes in the federal legislature, and therefore each vote will have an equal weight, whether coming from a large or a smaller state, or a state more or less wealthy or powerful. It will be just as in the case of a state legislature, where the representatives of unequal counties or other districts have an exact equality of value and influence. If a state representative does have any unequal influence, it stems from the difference in his personal character rather than any regard to the size of his district."

These are the arguments that an advocate for the southern interests might make on this subject. Although some of them may seem weak, on the whole I must admit that they fully reconcile me to the scale of representation which the convention has established.

In one respect, the establishment of a common measure for representation and taxation will have a very beneficial effect. Because the accuracy of the census to be obtained by Congress will necessarily depend in large part on the cooperation of the states, it is very important that the states be as little biased as possible toward inflating or downplaying the amount of their numbers. If only their share of representation were to be governed by this rule, they would have an interest in exaggerating their inhabitants. If only their share of taxation were to be governed by the rule, the opposite temptation would exist. By extending the rule to both, the states will have conflicting interests which will check and balance each other, producing the necessary impartiality.

Federalist 57

[Madison]

The third charge against the House of Representatives is that its members will be derived from that class of citizens which will have the least sympathy with the majority of the people, and be most likely to ambitiously sacrifice the many for the advancement of the few.

Of all the objections which have been made against the federal Constitution, this is perhaps the most extraordinary. While the objection itself is directed against an imaginary oligarchy, its principle strikes at the very root of republican government.

The goal of every political constitution is, or should be, twofold: first, to obtain for rulers the men who possess the most wisdom to perceive, and the most virtue to pursue, the common good of the society; and secondly, to make the most effective precautions for keeping them virtuous while they continue to hold their public trust.[1] Elections are the usual way in which rulers are obtained in republican governments. The means that such governments rely on to prevent the corruption of these rulers are numerous and various. The most effective one is a definite term of appointment, which is designed to maintain a proper responsibility to the people.

Let me now ask: What circumstance is there in the constitution of the House of Representatives that violates the principles of republican government, or that favors the elevation of the few on the ruins of the many? Isn't every circumstance, on the contrary, strictly aligned with these principles, and carefully unbiased toward the rights of every class and type of citizen?

Who are to be the electors of the federal representatives? Not the rich any more than the poor, not the educated any more than the uneducated, not the members of prominent families any more than the common man. The electors are to be the great body of the people of the United States. They are to be the same people who exercise the right of electing the corresponding branch of the legislature in their state.

Who are to be the representatives elected by these people? Every citizen whose merit inspires the admiration and confidence of his country. No qualification of wealth, of birth, of religious faith, or of profession is allowed to constrain the judgment or frustrate the preference of the people.

If we consider the situation of the representatives once elected, we will find that it includes every security which can be designed or desired for their responsibility to their constituents.

In the first place, we may presume that in general they will actually possess those qualities which led their fellow citizens to choose them, and which promise a sincere and careful respect for the nature of their office.

Secondly, they will enter into public service under circumstances which will certainly produce at least a temporary affection for their constituents. Everyone is sensitive to the recognition, esteem, and confidence of their peers, which is by itself some motivation for showing gratitude and benevolence in return. Ingratitude is, it is true, often listed as a common failing of human nature, and instances of it are too frequent and obvious both in public and in private life. But the universal and extreme disapproval which ingratitude inspires is itself a proof of the power and persistence of the opposite feeling.

Thirdly, the ties binding the representative to his constituents are also strengthened by more selfish motives. His pride and vanity will attach him to a form of government which furthers his ambitions and gives him a share in its honors and distinctions. Whatever hopes or projects might be entertained by a few aspiring individuals, in general those who derive their advancement from their influence with the people would have more to gain from a preservation of the people's approval than from a subversion of the people's authority.

All of these securities, however, would not be enough without the restraint of frequent elections. Therefore, fourthly, the House of Representatives is designed so as to continually remind the members of their dependence on the people. Before their feelings of gratitude and affection toward their constituents can be worn off by the exercise of power, they will be forced to look ahead to the moment when their power will cease, when their exercise of this power is to be judged, and when they must descend back to the level of the people from which they were raised—there forever to remain unless a responsible exercise of their trust will have earned its renewal.

Fifthly, I will add that members of the House of Representatives can make no law which will not apply as fully to themselves and their friends as to the great body of society. This has always been considered one of the strongest bonds by which human policy can connect the rulers and the people together. It creates between them that agreement of interests and sympathy of feelings which is rare in any government, but without which every government becomes a tyranny. If one were to ask: What is to prevent the House of Representatives from making legal discriminations in favor of themselves and the elite class of society? I answer: the design of the whole system, the nature of fair and constitutional laws, and above all, the vigilant and active spirit which animates the people of America—a spirit which sustains freedom, and is in turn sustained by it.

If this spirit is ever so far weakened as to tolerate a law that does not apply to the members of the legislature equally with the people, the people will be prepared to tolerate anything but liberty.

Such will be the relationship between the House of Representatives and their constituents. Duty, gratitude, interest, and ambition itself are the ties which will bind them to responsibility and sympathy with the people. It is, of course, possible that these may all be insufficient to control the whims and wickedness of human nature. But are they not all that government will allow for, and that human intelligence can design? Are they not the genuine and the usual means by which republican government provides for the liberty and happiness of the people? Are they not the identical means on which every state government in the Union relies for attaining these important goals? What, then, are we to understand by the objection which this paper has argued against? What are we to say to those who profess the most passionate zeal for republican government, and yet boldly question its fundamental principle? Who pretend to be champions for the right and ability of the people to elect their own rulers, and yet argue that these people will usually prefer representatives who will immediately betray their trust?

If this objection were heard by someone who hadn't seen the mode of election prescribed by the Constitution for representatives, he would assume that there was some unreasonable property qualification required for voting rights, or that only wealthy persons from prominent families were allowed to run for office, or at least that the Constitution had departed significantly from the mode of election prescribed by the state constitutions. We have already seen, though, that the first two assumptions are incorrect. And the last would be incorrect as well. The only apparent difference between the mode of election prescribed by the federal Constitution and those of the state constitutions is that each representative of the United States will be elected by five or six thousand citizens, while in the individual states the election of a representative is left to about five or six hundred. Would this difference be sufficient to justify an attachment to the state governments and a mistrust of the federal government? If this is the crucial point of the objection, it deserves to be examined.

Is it supported by *reason*? Are five or six thousand citizens less capable of choosing a good representative, or more likely to be fooled by a bad one, than five or six hundred? Reason, on the contrary, assures us both that a good representative would be most likely to be found among this larger number, and that the election would be less likely to be corrupted by political maneuvering or moneyed interests.

Can we allow the *consequence* of this doctrine? If we say that five or six hundred citizens are the maximum number who can be represented, wouldn't we have to deprive the people of voting rights in every case where the administration of the government does not require as many officials as the one-per-five-hundred rule would dictate?

Is the doctrine confirmed by *facts*? It was shown in the last paper that the real representation in the British House of Commons is in the proportion of about one for every thirty thousand inhabitants. In addition to a variety of powerful causes which favor the privileges of wealth and rank in that country, there are legal distinctions relating to representation as well. No person is able to serve as a representative of a county unless he possesses property valued at six hundred pounds sterling per year, nor of a city or borough unless he possesses three hundred pounds per year. To this qualification for the representatives is added another for the electors, which limits voting rights to persons owning property worth at least twenty pounds sterling per year. Despite these circumstances, and despite some very unequal laws in the British legal code, however, it still can't be said that the representatives of that nation have privileged the few at the expense of the many.

But we need not resort to foreign experience on this subject. Our own is clear and decisive. The districts in New Hampshire in which the senators are chosen directly by the people are almost as large as will be necessary for her representatives in Congress. Those of Massachusetts are larger than will be necessary for that purpose, and those of New York even more so. In New York the members of the Assembly for the cities and counties of New York and Albany are elected by almost as many voters as will be entitled to a representative in Congress (calculating on the number of sixty-five representatives only).

It makes no difference that in these senatorial districts and counties a number of representatives are voted for by each elector at the same time. If the same electors at the same time are capable of choosing four or five representatives, they can't be incapable of choosing one. Pennsylvania is another example. Some of her counties, which elect her state representatives, are almost as large as her federal representative districts will be. The city of Philadelphia contains between fifty and sixty thousand people. It will therefore form nearly two districts for electing federal representatives. It forms, however, a single county, in which every elector votes for each of its representatives in the state legislature. And, moreover, the whole city actually elects a *single member* for the executive council. This is the case in all the other counties of the state.

Aren't these facts adequate refutation of the false argument which has been used against the proposed House of Representatives? Has it been shown by experience that the senators of New Hampshire, Massachusetts, and New York, or the executive council of Pennsylvania, or the members of the Assembly in New York and Pennsylvania, have tended to sacrifice the many to the few, or are in any way less deserving of their places than the representatives chosen in other states by very small districts?

And there are even more extreme cases than those which I have referenced. In one branch of the Connecticut legislature, each member is elected by the whole state. So is the governor of Connecticut, of

Massachusetts, and New York, as well as the president of New Hampshire. I leave to the reader to decide whether our experience in any of these cases supports a suspicion that large electoral districts tend to bring traitors into power and to undermine the public liberty.

Federalist 62

[Madison]

Having examined the design of the House of Representatives and answered the most important objections against it, I proceed to examine the Senate.

The headings under which I will consider the design of the Senate are: (1) the qualifications of senators; (2) the appointment of them by the state legislatures; (3) the equality of representation in the Senate; (4) the number of senators and their term length; and (5) the Senate's powers.

(1) The qualifications proposed for senators, as opposed to those of representatives in the House, consist in a higher minimum age and a longer required period of citizenship. A senator must be thirty years of age at least, and a representative in the House must be twenty-five. A senator must have been a citizen for nine years, and a representative in the House only seven years. The need for these differences is explained by the particular function of the Senate, which requires in its members greater extent of information and stability of character, qualities which require in turn that the senator should have reached a time of life most likely to supply them. The function of the Senate also involves participating directly in transactions with foreign nations, which should be done only by those who do not still possess the predispositions and habits that accompany foreign birth and education. The period of nine years seems to be a happy medium between a total exclusion of adopted citizens whose merits and talents may suit them for public office, and an indiscriminate and hasty inclusion of them, which might open up a channel for foreign influence on Congress.

(2) It is equally unnecessary to discuss the appointment of senators by the state legislatures at great length. Among the various means for choosing senators which might have been adopted, that which the convention has proposed is probably the least controversial. It has the double advantage of encouraging an elite appointment, and of giving the state governments an

influence in the federal government which will both secure their authority and form a convenient link between the two systems.

(3) The equality of representation in the Senate is another point which does not call for much discussion, since it was obviously the result of compromise between the opposite interests of the large and the small states. If it is right that (a) among a people thoroughly joined into one nation, every part ought to have a share in the government *proportional* to their population; and that, (b) on the other hand, among independent and sovereign states joined by a treaty, each state should have an *equal* share in the common congress, it seems plausible that (c) in a republic neither wholly national nor wholly federal, the government ought to be founded on a mixture of proportional and equal representation (the House and the Senate).

But it is pointless to hold this part of the Constitution up to any theoretical analysis, since it is admitted by everyone to be the result, not of theory, but "of a spirit of amity, and that mutual deference and concession which the peculiarity of our political situation rendered indispensable." A common government with powers equal to its obligations is called for by the voice and, especially, the political situation of America. A government founded on principles of representation more in agreement with the wishes of the larger states is not likely to be consented to by the smaller states. The only option then, for the larger states, lies between the proposed government and an even worse one. Given this alternative, it is most prudent to embrace the lesser evil. And instead of speculating about the possible problems which may arise from the compromise, we should focus on the beneficial consequences which might counterbalance them.

Along these lines it may be said that the equal vote given to each state in the Senate is both a constitutional recognition of the portion of sovereignty remaining in the individual states, and a tool for preserving that remaining sovereignty. In this way the equality ought to be no less acceptable to the large than to the small states, since they are just as careful to guard in every way against an improper consolidation of the states into one simple republic.

Another benefit from this ingredient in the constitution of the Senate is the additional obstacle it will put up against unfair legislation. No law or resolution can now be passed without the agreement of both a majority of the people and a majority of the states. I admit that this complicated check on legislation may in some cases be harmful as well as beneficial. The particular defense which it involves in favor of the smaller states would be more rational if these small states had any common and unique interests which might otherwise be in danger. But because (a) the larger states will always be able, by their power over the supplies, to defeat unreasonable uses of this checking by the smaller states, and because (b) the ease and excess of lawmaking seem to be the usual faults of our governments, it is not impossible that (c) this part of the Constitution may be less problematic in practice than it appears to many in theory.

(4) The number of senators and their term length is the next topic to be considered. In order to understand both of these points, it will be necessary to specify the purposes which the Senate is designed to serve. And in order to specify these, it will be necessary to explain the difficulties which a republic would suffer in the absence of such an institution.

First: It is a problem for republican governments, though less so than for other governments, that politicians may forget their obligations to their constituents and prove unfaithful to their important trust. Looked at this way, a senate, as a second branch of the legislature which is distinct from, and shares power with, a first, must always be a helpful check on the government. It doubles the security to the people,[1] by requiring the agreement of two distinct representative bodies in corrupt or underhanded schemes, where the ambition or corruption of one would otherwise be enough. This is a precaution based on such clear principles, and by now so well understood throughout the United States, that there is no need to elaborate on it. I will only say that, because the effectiveness of this precaution will increase as the differences between the two representative bodies increase, it makes sense to differentiate them from each other as much as possible, without at the same time disrupting necessary harmony on appropriate measures or violating the principles of republican government.

Secondly: The necessity of a senate is also suggested by the tendency of all single and numerous legislative assemblies to give in to the impulse of sudden and violent passions, and to be tricked by factious leaders into rash and dangerous resolutions. Many examples of this might be given, both from the United States as well as from the history of other nations. But a statement that will not be denied doesn't need to be proved. All that needs to be said is that a representative body which is to correct this problem should itself be free from it, and therefore should be a less numerous one. It should, moreover, possess great firmness, and therefore should hold its authority for a considerably longer term.

Thirdly: Another difficulty which may be answered by a senate lies in a lack of sufficient familiarity with the objects and principles of legislation. It is not possible that an assembly of men called for the most part from private business, having only a short time in office, and probably not devoting their free time to studying the laws, issues, and interests of their country, should by themselves avoid a variety of important mistakes in the exercise of their legislative trust. It may be very confidently stated that a large part of the current embarrassments of America is due to the mistakes of our governments, and that these mistakes have proceeded from the heads rather than the hearts of our representatives. What are all of the repealing, explaining, and amending laws which fill and disgrace our extensive legal codes, but so many witnesses of deficient wisdom? What are they but so many condemnations of each legislative session against the preceding one? What are they but so many confirmations to the people of the value of a well-designed senate?

A good government implies two things: first, fidelity to the goal of government, which is the happiness of the people; and secondly, a knowledge of the means by which that goal can best be reached.[2] Some governments are deficient in both of these qualities; most governments are deficient in the first. I don't hesitate to assert that in American governments too little attention has been paid to the second. The federal Constitution avoids this error; and what deserves particular notice is that it provides for the second in a way that increases the security for the first.

Fourthly: The frequent changes in legislation arising from a frequent change of members, however qualified they may be, shows clearly the necessity of some stable institution in the government. Every new election in the states changes half of the representatives. From this change of representatives must follow a change of opinions; and from a change of opinions, a change of measures. But a frequent change even of good measures is both imprudent and counterproductive. This is true in private life, and becomes more applicable and important in the public life of a nation.

Tracing the negative effects of a constantly changing government would fill a book. I will indicate just a few, each of which will be seen to be a source of many more.

In the first place, it lessens the respect and trust of other nations, and all the advantages connected with national character. An individual who is observed to be inconsistent in his plans, or perhaps to live his life without any plan at all, is noticed at once by all prudent people as one who is likely to be a speedy victim to his own inconsistency and foolishness. His more friendly neighbors may pity him, but all will avoid connecting their fortunes with his, and many will seize the opportunity of making their fortunes out of his. One nation is to another what one individual is to another; with the possible difference that nations, possessing fewer benevolent emotions than individuals, are less likely to feel restrained from taking unfair advantage of each other's mistakes.

As a result of this, every nation whose affairs show a lack of wisdom and stability can count on suffering every loss which can result from the more systematic policies of their wiser neighbors. But the best education on this subject has been unfortunately given to America by the example of her own situation. She finds that she is held in no respect by her friends, that she is the mockery of her enemies, and that she is a victim to every nation which has an interest in benefiting from her frequently changing policies and embarrassed affairs.

The internal effects of frequently changing policy are even more disastrous. It poisons the blessing of liberty itself. It will be of little use to the people that the laws are made by men of their own choice, if the laws are so lengthy that they cannot be read, or so incoherent that they cannot be understood; if they are repealed or revised before they are made known, or undergo such frequent changes that no one who knows what the law is today can guess what it will be tomorrow. Law is defined as a rule of action; but how can it be a rule if it is relatively unknown and frequently changing?[3]

Another effect of unstable legislation is the unreasonable advantage it gives to the clever, the enterprising, and the moneyed few over the hardworking and uninformed majority of the people. Every new regulation concerning commerce or revenue, or in any way affecting the value of different kinds of property, offers a reward to those who watch the change and can determine its consequences. This reward, though, is produced not by themselves, but by the work and effort of the great body of their fellow citizens. This is a state of things in which it may be accurately said that laws are made for the *few*, not for the *many*.

There is yet another way in which great injury results from an unstable government. A lack of confidence in public policy discourages every useful undertaking, because its success and profit may depend upon the continuance of existing arrangements. What prudent merchant will risk his wealth in any new branch of commerce when he doesn't know if his plans will be made unlawful before they can be carried out? What farmer or manufacturer will exert himself due to the encouragement given to any particular crop or business, when he has no guarantee that his work and progress will not fall victim to an unstable government? In short, no great improvement or admirable enterprise can move forward which requires an environment of stable public policy.

But the worst effect of all is that weakening of attachment and respect which enters into the hearts of the people toward a political system which shows so many signs of instability and disappoints so many of their hopes.

No government, any more than an individual, will long be respected without being truly respectable; and no government can be truly respectable without having a certain amount of order and stability.[4]

Federalist 68

[Hamilton]

The mode of appointment of the President of the United States is almost the only important part of the system which has escaped without serious criticism, or which has received the slightest sign of approval from its opponents. The most plausible of these opposing writings which has appeared in print ("Federal Farmer") even admits that the election of the President is pretty well provided for. I would go even further and affirm that if this mode of election is not perfect, it is at least excellent. It effectively brings together all of the elements one would wish for in the mode of election for this office.

It was desirable that public opinion should have an influence in the choice of the person who was to be given such an important trust. This goal will be achieved by giving the right of making the choice to men chosen by the people for the special purpose and at the particular time, rather than to any preexisting representative body.

It was equally desirable that the election be made directly by men most capable of analyzing the qualities needed for the office, and acting under circumstances favorable to deliberation and to a careful weighing of all the reasons and influences which should guide their choice. A small number of persons, selected by their fellow citizens from the great body of the people, will be most likely to possess the information and intelligence necessary for such complicated investigations.[1]

It was also particularly desirable to reduce the risk of upheaval and disorder at the time of election as far as possible. This evil was particularly to be feared in the election of a magistrate who was to have such an important role in the administration of the government as the President of the United States. But the precautions which have been so effectively implemented in the system under consideration promise an adequate security against this potential evil. The choice of *several* to form an intermediate group of electors will be much less likely to cause any upheaval in the community than the choice of *one* who would himself be the ultimate embodiment of public opinion. And because the electors chosen in each state are to assemble and vote in that state, this separated and divided situation will make them much less prone to dangerous passions which might be communicated from them to the people, than if they were all assembled at one time and in one place.

Nothing was more desirable than that every practicable obstacle should be set up against conspiracy, intrigue, and corruption. These most deadly enemies of republican government might originate from multiple sources, but would be expected to come particularly from the desire of foreign powers to gain a powerful agent in our government. How could they better carry out this purpose than by raising a spy of their own to the chief magistracy of the Union? But the convention has very carefully guarded against all dangers of this kind. They have not made the appointment of the President to depend on any preexisting bodies of men, who might be tampered with beforehand to sell their votes. Instead, they have made the election of the President to originate from the people of America in choosing persons for the temporary and sole purpose of making the ultimate election.

And they have excluded from eligibility all those who from their situation might be suspected of too great a devotion to the President in office. No senator, representative, or other person holding an office of trust or profit under the United States can be one of the electors. Therefore the direct electors of the President will at least enter upon their task free from any sinister bias, and won't be expected to corrupt the great body of the people while carrying out this task. Their temporary existence and their detached situation make it likely that they will continue in this manner to the conclusion of the election. The business of corruption, when it is to include such a large number of conspirators, requires time as well as means. And because the electors are spread out across the thirteen states, it wouldn't be easy for them to suddenly form any alliances based on improper motives of any kind.

Another and equally important consideration was that the President should be dependent only on the people themselves for his reelection.[2] Otherwise, he might be tempted to sacrifice his duty to please those whose support was necessary to obtain reelection. This is another advantage that will be secured by making his reelection dependent on a special representative body elected by the people for the single purpose of making this important choice.

All of these advantages will be combined in the convention's proposed plan: the people of each state will choose a number of persons as electors—

equal to the number of senators and representatives the state possesses in the national government—who will assemble within the state and cast their votes for President. Their votes are to be transmitted to the national capital, and the person who has a majority of votes will be the President. But because it may happen that no candidate receives a majority of the votes, and because it might be unsafe to allow less than a majority to be conclusive, the convention's plan provides that, in this case, the House of Representatives will select the man who in their opinion is best qualified for the office out of the five candidates with the highest number of votes.

This process of election makes it certain that the office of President will never be filled by any man who does not possess the necessary qualifications to a very high degree.[3] Talents for political tricks and techniques for gaining popularity may be enough to elevate a man to be governor of a single state. But it will require other talents, and a different kind of merit, for him to obtain the esteem and confidence of the whole Union, or of the substantial portion of it necessary to be elected President of the United States. There will be a constant probability of seeing the position filled by individuals who are known to excel in ability and virtue. And because the executive in every government plays a considerable role in its good or ill administration, this is an important point in the Constitution's favor. Although we cannot agree with the political heresy of the poet who says:

> "For forms of government let fools contest—
> That which is best administered is best,"—

yet we may safely say that the true test of a good government is its ability and tendency to produce a good administration.

The Vice President is to be chosen in the same manner as the President. The only difference in this case is that the Senate is to play the same role with respect to the election of the Vice President that the House of Representatives plays with respect to the election of the President.

The appointment of a special person as Vice President has been objected to as unnecessary, if not dangerous. It has been argued that it would have been preferable to have authorized the Senate to elect a Vice President from among themselves. But two considerations seem to justify the ideas of the convention on this point. One is, that to guarantee at all times the possibility of a definite decision of the body, it is necessary that the president of the Senate should have only a casting vote in case of a tie. And to take the senator of any state from his seat as senator, and to make him president of the Senate, would be a disadvantage for the state he represents by exchanging his constant vote for a contingent one. The other consideration is that, because the Vice President may occasionally become the President, all the reasons which support the mode of election for the President apply with great if not with equal force to the mode of election for the Vice President.

It is remarkable that in this, as in most other instances, the objection which is made would run contrary to the constitution of this state. We have a lieutenant governor who is president of the state senate, and is the constitutional substitute for the governor in cases similar to those which would authorize the Vice President to exercise the authorities and discharge the duties of the President, and this lieutenant governor is elected by the people at large rather than the Senate themselves.

Federalist 70

[Hamilton]

Some argue for the idea that an efficient Executive is inconsistent with the spirit of republican government. The enlightened friends of republican government must at least hope that this idea is incorrect, since they can't admit its truth without at the same time undermining their own principles. Efficiency in the Executive is a primary feature of good government. It is essential to national security, to the consistent enforcement of the laws, to the protection of property against movements to disrupt the ordinary course of justice, and to the security of liberty against assaults of ambition, of faction, and of anarchy. Everyone who is familiar with Roman history knows how often that republic needed to give absolute power to a single dictator in order to protect against internal conspiracies and seditions as well as external invasions.

There is no need, however, to multiply arguments or examples along these lines. A weak Executive implies a weak execution of the government. Weak execution is just another way of saying bad execution, and a government poorly executed, whatever it may be in theory, must in practice be a bad government.[1]

Admitting, therefore, that everyone of sense will agree on the necessity of an efficient Executive, it only remains to ask: What ingredients constitute this efficiency? To what extent can they be combined with the ingredients which constitute republican safety? And how far does this combination characterize the convention's plan?

The ingredients which constitute efficiency in the Executive are, first, unity; secondly, duration; thirdly, an adequate provision for its support; and fourthly, competent powers.

The ingredients which constitute republican safety are, first, a sufficient dependence on the people; and secondly, a sufficient responsibility to the people.

Those politicians and statesmen who have been the most celebrated for the soundness of their principles and for the justice of their views have favored a single Executive and a numerous legislature. They have rightly considered efficiency as the most necessary qualification of the Executive, and have judged this to be most attainable by a single hand. They have, with equal correctness, considered a numerous legislature as best suited to deliberation and wisdom, and best designed to win the confidence of the people and to secure their privileges and interests.

No one will deny that unity leads to efficiency. Decision, activity, secrecy, and effectiveness will usually be more characteristic of one man than of any greater number, and as the number is increased these qualities will decrease.

This unity may be destroyed in two ways: either by giving power to two or more magistrates of equal position and authority; or by giving it to one man but subjecting him to the control and cooperation of a council. The two consuls of Rome may serve as an example of the first; the constitutions of several of the states provide examples of the second. New York and New Jersey, if I remember correctly, are the only states which give the executive authority entirely to a single man. Both methods of destroying the unity of the Executive have their proponents, but those in favor of an executive council are the most numerous. Because both are open to similar objections, they may largely be examined together.

The experience of other nations give us little help on this subject. Insofar as it teaches us anything, though, it teaches us not to prefer a plurality in the Executive. We have seen that the Achaeans, after trying two praetors, were led to abolish one. The Roman history relates many instances of danger to the republic from the disagreements between the consuls, and between the military tribunes who were at times substituted for the consuls. But this history gives us no examples of any particular advantages given to the state from the fact of their having more than one executive magistrate.

It is astonishing that the struggles between the consuls were not more frequent or more troublesome. This was due to the unique position of the republic, and to the prudent policy indicated by the circumstances of the state, and pursued by the consuls, of dividing the government between them. The patricians were constantly engaged in a struggle with the plebeians for the preservation of their ancient authorities and privileges, and the consuls—who were generally chosen from among the patricians—were commonly united by the personal interest they had in defending the patricians' privileges. In addition to this motive of union, the expansion of the republic through conquest led to an established custom of dividing the administration of the government between the two consuls by lot. One of them would remain at Rome to govern the city and its surrounding areas, and the other would take command in the more distant provinces. This custom must, no doubt, have had great influence in preventing those disagreements and struggles which might otherwise have ruined the peace of the republic.

But leaving the dim light of historical research and using only our reason and good sense, we will find much greater cause to reject than to approve the idea of plurality in the Executive, no matter how this plurality is constructed.

Whenever two or more persons are engaged in any common enterprise or pursuit, there is always danger of a difference of opinion. If this common pursuit is a public trust or office, in which they are given equal dignity and authority, there is a particular danger of personal rivalry and even animosity. From either, and especially from all of these causes, the most intense conflicts tend to arise. Whenever these happen, they lessen the respectability, weaken the authority, and hinder the plans and operations of those whom they divide. If they should happen in the supreme executive magistracy of a country, they might block or frustrate the most important functions of the government in the most critical emergencies of the state. And what is even worse, they might split the community into polarized factions, each attached to the different individuals who compose the magistracy.

Human beings often oppose something merely because they have had no role in planning it, or because it was planned by those whom they dislike. And if they have been consulted, and happened to disapprove, opposition then becomes to them a duty of self-love. They seem to think that they are duty-bound, and by all the motives of personal infallibility, to defeat the success of a plan that has been decided upon against their opposition. Those of upright and benevolent character often remark, with horror, on the desperate lengths to which this disposition is sometimes carried. Often, in such cases, the great interests of society are sacrificed to the vanity, the pride, and the stubbornness of individuals who have enough celebrity to make their passions and whims interesting to mankind. The current debate over the proposed Constitution offers unfortunate evidence of the effects of this despicable weakness, or rather detestable vice, in human nature.

According to the principles of free government, the legislature cannot avoid the inconveniences stemming from this vice. But it is unnecessary, and therefore unwise, to introduce these inconveniences into the constitution of the Executive. It is, moreover, in the Executive that they may be most dangerous.

In the legislature, speediness of decision is more often an evil than a benefit. Differences of opinion and party conflicts in that department of the government, though they may sometimes hinder good plans, yet often promote deliberation and caution, as well as provide a check on excesses in the majority. And once a resolution is made, the opposition must end. That resolution is a law, and resistance to it is punishable.

But no positive effects make up for the disadvantages of disagreement and conflict in the executive department. Here, the disadvantages are pure and simple. There is no point at which they cease to operate. They serve to embarrass and weaken the execution of every plan or measure they affect from its first step to its final conclusion. They constantly act against the most necessary ingredients in the composition of the Executive—vigor and effectiveness—and they do this without offering any good on the other side. In the conduct of war, in which the efficiency of the Executive is crucial for national security, we would have everything to fear from the disadvantages of a plurality in the Executive.

It must be admitted that these observations apply primarily to the first method of making a plural Executive—that is, to a plurality of magistrates of equal position and authority—and the advocates of this option are not likely to form a very numerous group. But they apply also to the second method of a council whose consent is made constitutionally necessary to the operations of the ostensible Executive. A secret conspiracy in that council would be able to derail and weaken the whole system of administration. Even in the absence of such a conspiracy, mere differences of views and opinions would alone be enough to taint the exercise of the executive authority with a spirit of habitual weakness and sluggishness.

But one of the most serious objections to a plurality in the Executive, and which applies equally to the first and the second methods, is that it tends to hide faults and destroy responsibility. Responsibility is of two kinds—to public disapproval and to legal punishment. The first is more important, especially in an elective office. Human beings given public trust will much more often act in an untrustworthy manner than in an illegal manner. But the multiplication of the Executive adds to the difficulty of detection in either case. It often becomes impossible, amid mutual accusations, to determine where the blame or punishment for harmful measures should fall. It is shifted from one to another with so much skill and plausibility that the public opinion is left in suspense about the real author of the measure. The circumstances which may have led to any national misfortune are sometimes so complicated, and the number of politicians who may have played a role in them so numerous, that, though we may clearly see that there has been mismanagement, it is impossible to charge the evil to any one of them.

"I was overruled by my council. The council was so divided that it was impossible to obtain any better decision on the point." These and similar excuses are constantly available, whether true or false. And who will either take the time or risk the notoriety of conducting a strict investigation into the hidden causes of the trouble? And if there is a citizen zealous enough to undertake this unpromising task, how easy would it be for politicians to collude among themselves and make the circumstances so ambiguous as to render the precise actions of any of them uncertain?

In the single instance in which the governor of New York is joined to a council—that is, in the appointment to offices—we have seen these problems. Scandalous appointments to important offices have been made. Some cases have even been so flagrant that all parties have agreed on their impropriety. When investigations have been made, the blame has been placed by the governor on the members of the council, who in turn have placed it on the governor. The people, meanwhile, remain completely at a loss to determine by whose influence their interests have been entrusted to people so unqualified and so obviously improper. Out of respect for individuals, I won't go into particulars.

It is clear from these considerations that the plurality of the Executive tends to deprive the people of the two greatest securities they can have for the faithful exercise of any delegated power. The *first* of these is the restraints of public opinion, which lose their effectiveness both because of the division of disapproval for bad measures among a number of individuals, and because of the uncertainty regarding who these individuals should be. And the *second* is the ability to discover easily and clearly the misconduct of the persons they trust, in order to either remove them from office or charge them with actual crimes.

In England, the king is a perpetual magistrate. For the sake of public peace, the rule has been adopted that he is unaccountable for his administration and his person is sacred. It is very wise in that kingdom, therefore, to give the king a constitutional council who may be responsible to the nation for the advice they give him. Without this, there would be no responsibility whatsoever in the executive department—an idea that is inadmissible in a free government. But even there the king is not bound by the resolutions of his council, although they are responsible for the advice they give. He is the absolute master of his own conduct in the exercise of his office, and may follow or disregard the advice given to him at his sole discretion.

But in a republic, where every magistrate ought to be personally responsible for his behavior in office, the reason which makes a council desirable in the British Constitution not only ceases to apply, but actually speaks against such a council. In the monarchy of Great Britain, it supplies a substitute for the king's lack of responsibility, and serves in some degree to secure his good behavior. In the American republic, it would serve to destroy, or at least greatly diminish, the intended and necessary responsibility of the President himself.

The idea of a council to the Executive, which has generally been adopted by the state constitutions, has been derived from the republican rule that power is safer in the hands of many than in the hands of one. Even admitting the rule to be applicable in this case, I would argue that the advantage in terms of safety would not outweigh the numerous disadvantages on the other side. But I do not think the rule at all applicable to the executive power. I agree on this point with a writer whom the celebrated Junius calls "deep, solid, and ingenious," that "the executive power is more easily confined when it is ONE." It is far safer for there to be a single object for the suspicion and careful observation of the people. In short, all multiplication of the Executive is dangerous rather than friendly to liberty.

A brief consideration should satisfy us that the kind of security sought for in the multiplication of the Executive is unattainable. The number must be so great as to render the formation of a faction difficult; otherwise it will be more a source of danger than of security. The united fame and influence of several individuals must be more dangerous to liberty than the fame and influence of any of them separately. When power, therefore, is placed in the hands of a small enough number of individuals that their interests and views may be easily joined in a common enterprise by a skillful leader, this power becomes more open to abuse, and is more dangerous when it is abused, than if it is placed in the hands of one individual. This is because the single individual, from the very circumstance of his being alone, will be more carefully watched and more quickly suspected.

He will also be incapable of exerting as much influence by himself as he is able to in association with others.

The decemvirs of Rome, whose name indicates their number (ten), were more feared in their usurpation than any ONE of them would have been. No one would think of proposing an Executive much more numerous than this; from six to a dozen have been suggested for the number of the council. Even a dozen, though, is not too many for the easy formation of a faction; and from such a faction America would have more to fear than from the ambition of any single individual. A council to a magistrate, who is himself responsible for his actions, are generally nothing better than a clog upon his good intentions, are often the tools and accomplices of his bad intentions, and almost always hide his faults from public view.[2]

I won't dwell upon the subject of expense, though it is clear that if the council is to be numerous enough to serve its primary function, the salaries of the members, who must reside in the capital, would be too great an expense to be incurred for something of such debatable utility. I will only add that, prior to the appearance of the proposed Constitution, I rarely met with an intelligent man from any of the states who did not admit, as the result of experience, that the UNITY of the executive of this state (New York) was one of the best distinguishing features of our constitution.

Federalist 71

[Hamilton]

Duration in office has been mentioned as the second requirement for the effectiveness of the Executive authority. This factor affects two relevant characteristics of Executive authority: the decisiveness of the executive magistrate in the use of his constitutional powers, and the stability of the administrative system which may have been adopted under his leadership. With respect to the first, it is clear that the longer the time in office, the greater will be the probability of obtaining such an important characteristic. It is a general principle of human nature that a man's interest in whatever he has will be in proportion to the permanent or temporary nature of his holding it. He will be less attached to what he holds by a short and uncertain title than to what he enjoys by a longer or certain title—and, of course, he will be willing to risk more for the sake of the one than for the sake of the other. This principle is equally applicable to a political privilege, honor, or trust as it is to any article of ordinary property. The implication for us is that if a man acting as chief magistrate knows that in a very short time he *must* give up his office, he will tend to feel too little invested in it to risk any significant disapproval or misunderstanding resulting from the independent exercise of his powers. And he will be hesitant to provoke the anger, however temporary, which may happen to come about either in a substantial part of the society itself, or even in a dominant faction of the legislative body. If the case should only be that he *might* give up his office, unless he is reelected, his hopes for reelection would join with his fears to even more powerfully corrupt his integrity or weaken his courage. In either case, weakness and indecision must be the characteristics of the office.

There are some who tend to regard the submissive agreement of the Executive with the prevailing opinion, either in the community or in the legislature, as its best feature. But such people have very undeveloped ideas about the purposes of government and the means for promoting public happiness. The republican principle does demand that the deliberate sense of the community should govern the behavior of those to whom they entrust the management of their affairs. But this principle does not require strict compliance to every sudden breeze of passion, or to every passing impulse which might be implanted in the people by those who would flatter them in order to betray their own best interests.[1]

It is true that the people usually *intend* the PUBLIC GOOD. This is often the case even when they are wrong. But their good sense would despise the flatterer who would pretend that they always *reason rightly* about the *means* of promoting this good. The people know from experience that they are sometimes wrong, and it is amazing that they are so seldom wrong given the continuous deceptions of parasites and sycophants, the tricks of the ambitious, the greedy, and the desperate, and the maneuverings of politicians who have or seek the people's trust without deserving it. When occasions arise in which the best interests of the people are opposed to their short-term preferences, it is the duty of statesmen to withstand the temporary delusion of the people in order to give them time and opportunity for more calm and careful reflection. Examples could be given in which the carrying out of this duty has saved the people from the fatal consequences of their own mistakes, securing in the process the lasting gratitude of the people toward the statesmen who had the courage and vision to serve them at the risk of incurring their disapproval or anger.

But even if we were to insist upon the submissive agreement of the Executive with public opinion, we shouldn't argue for a similar agreement with the prevailing opinions in the legislature. These opinions may sometimes stand in opposition to public opinion, and at other times the people may be entirely neutral with respect to them. In either case, it is certainly desirable that the Executive should feel able to act on his own opinion with vigor and decisiveness.

The same rule which dictates a separation between the various branches of government, dictates also that this separation ought to be designed to make the one independent of the other. Why separate the executive or the judiciary from the legislative, if they are so designed as to be subject to it? Such a separation must be merely superficial, and incapable of achieving the goals for which it was established. It is one thing to be subordinate to the laws, and another to be subordinate to the legislative body. The first agrees with the fundamental principles of good government and the second violates them by uniting all power in the same hands.

The tendency of the legislative authority to absorb every other has been fully explained and established by examples in earlier essays. In purely republican governments, this tendency is almost irresistible. The representatives of the people in a popular assembly seem sometimes to think that they are the people themselves. Because of this, they tend to become impatient and disgusted at the least sign of opposition from any other part of the government, as if the exercise of executive or judicial rights were a violation of legislative privilege and offensive to their dignity. They often appear disposed to exercise an arrogant control over the other departments, and since they commonly have the people on their side, they always act with such momentum as to make it very difficult for the other members of the government to maintain the Constitutional balance.

It may be asked how the shortness of time in office can affect the independence of the Executive from the legislature, unless the one had the power of appointing or removing the other. One answer to this question may be drawn from the principle already mentioned—that is, from the slight interest a man tends to take in a short-lived advantage, and the little motivation it gives him to undertake any substantial inconvenience or risk. Another and perhaps more obvious answer, though not more convincing, comes from considering the influence of the legislative body over the people. This influence might be used to block the reelection of someone who, by a courageous resistance to any sinister project of the legislature, should have brought on their resentment.

It may be asked also whether a duration of four years would be enough to achieve this goal of decisiveness and independence. And if it would not, it may be asked whether a shorter period, which would provide greater security against ambitious plots of the Executive, would not therefore be preferable.

It cannot be claimed that a duration of four years, or any other period of time, would completely achieve the goal proposed. It would, though, contribute toward achieving this goal to a degree which would have a significant influence upon the spirit and character of the government. Between the beginning and end of a four-year period, there would be a substantial interval in which the prospect of leaving office would be far enough away to not have a negative effect on the conduct of a moderately courageous man. During this interval he might reasonably think to himself that there would be enough time to convince the community of the beneficial nature of the measures he would like to pursue before the time for leaving office would arrive. Although it is probable that, as he approached the time of possible reelection, his confidence and decisiveness would decline, yet both would derive support from the esteem and goodwill that he would have had the opportunity of winning from his constituents. He might, then, pursue important projects with confidence in proportion to the evidence he had given of his wisdom and integrity, and to the respect and attachment he had earned from his fellow citizens. A duration of four years will, then, contribute enough to the decisiveness and independence of the Executive to make it a very valuable ingredient in the composition of the office.

Nor will this duration be so long as to justify any fears for the public liberty. The British House of Commons, from the most humble beginnings (having the mere power of agreeing or disagreeing with a new tax), have rapidly reduced the power of the king and the privileges of the nobles within the limits they thought to be required by the principles of a free government. They have, at the same time, raised themselves to the rank and influence of a coequal branch of the legislature. They have been able, in one instance, to abolish both the royalty and the aristocracy, and to overturn all the old establishments both in the Church and the State. They have been able, recently, to make the king tremble at the fear of an attempted change. Considering this example, what reason do we have to fear an elected magistrate with a four-year term, and with the limited powers of a President of the United States? What do we have to fear except that he might not be equal to the task which the Constitution gives him? I will only add that if the length of his term leaves doubt about his decisiveness and independence, that doubt is inconsistent with a fear that he will abuse his power.

Federalist 78

[Hamilton]

We proceed now to an examination of the judiciary department of the proposed government.

In showing the defects of the existing Confederation, the utility and necessity of a federal judiciary have already been clearly pointed out. Nor is the institution controversial in the abstract; the only questions which have been raised relate to the manner of its design and to the extent of its authority. We will, then, keep our observations confined to these points.

The manner of its design seems to include these elements: (1) the mode of appointing the judges; (2) the tenure by which they are to hold their offices; and (3) the division of the judiciary authority between different courts, and their relations to each other.

(1) With respect to the mode of appointing the judges: this is the same as the mode of appointing the officers of the Union in general, and has been so fully discussed in previous essays that nothing new can be said here.

(2) With respect to the tenure by which the judges are to hold their places: this primarily concerns their duration in office, the provisions for their support while in office, and the precautions for their responsibility.

According to the convention's plan, all judges who may be appointed by the United States are to hold their offices *during good behavior*, which is the same duration prescribed by the best state constitutions, including the one of this state (New York). The fact that its appropriateness has been called into question by the enemies of the convention's plan is clear evidence of the animosity which disorders their imaginations and judgments. The standard of good behavior for judges is certainly one of the most valuable of the modern improvements in the practice of government. In a monarchy it is an excellent barrier to the oppression of the prince; in a republic it is an equally excellent barrier to the abuses of power and oppressions of the representative body. And it is the best tool which can be used in any government to secure a consistent, honorable, and unbiased administration of the laws.

Anyone who carefully considers the different departments of power must see that, in a government of separated powers, the judiciary, from the nature of its functions and the limitations of its capacities, will always be the least dangerous to the political rights of the Constitution.[1] The executive not only distributes honors, but holds the sword of the community. The legislature not only controls the budget, but makes the rules by which the duties and rights of every citizen are to be regulated. The judiciary, on the other hand, has no influence over either the sword or the purse—no direction either of the strength or of the wealth of the society—and can initiate no action whatsoever. It may truly be said to have neither FORCE nor WILL, but merely judgment; and it must ultimately depend upon the cooperation of the executive even for the enforcement of its judgments.

This simple description indicates several important consequences. It proves that the judiciary is by far the weakest of the three departments of power, that it can never attack either of the other two successfully, and that all possible care is necessary to enable it to defend itself against their attacks. It equally proves that although individual oppression may now and then proceed from the courts of justice, the general liberty of the people can never be endangered by them—at least as long as the judiciary remains truly distinct from both the legislative and the executive. For I agree that "there is no liberty, if the power of judging be not separated from the legislative and executive powers." And it proves, finally, that because (a) liberty has nothing to fear from the judiciary by itself, but would have everything to fear from its union with either of the other departments; because (b) all the effects of this union of powers must arise from a dependence of the judiciary on one of the others; because (c), from the natural weakness of the judiciary, it is in constant danger of being overpowered, intimidated, or influenced by the other branches; and because (d) nothing can contribute so much to the decisiveness and independence of the judiciary as a permanent appointment to office, this feature may therefore (e) be fairly regarded as an essential ingredient in its design, and, in large part, as the stronghold of public justice and security.

The complete independence of the courts of justice is particularly essential in a limited Constitution. By a limited Constitution, I mean one which contains certain specific exceptions to the legislative authority, such as that it shall pass no bills of attainder or *ex post facto* laws. Limitations of this kind can be preserved in practice only through courts of justice, whose duty it must be to declare all acts contrary to the clear meaning of the Constitution void. Without this, all the reservations of particular rights or privileges would amount to nothing.

Some confusion has arisen regarding the rights of courts to declare legislative acts void when they are contrary to the Constitution, because it seems to imply a superiority of the judiciary to the legislative power. It is argued that the authority which can declare the acts of another void must necessarily be superior to the one whose acts may be declared void. Because this right of the courts is of great importance in all the American constitutions, I will briefly discuss the reasons for it.

It is obvious that every act of a delegated authority that is contrary to the intention of its commission is void. No legislative act, therefore, can be valid if it is contrary to the Constitution. To deny this would be to affirm that the agent is greater than his principal, that the servant is above his master, that the representatives of the people are superior to the people themselves, and that those specifically empowered may do not only what their powers do not authorize, but what they forbid.

If it is argued that the legislative body are themselves the constitutional judges of their own powers, and that their interpretation of these powers is binding on the other departments, it may be answered that this cannot be the natural assumption when it is not indicated by any particular provisions in the Constitution. There are no grounds to suppose that the Constitution could intend to enable the representatives of the people to substitute their *will* for that of their constituents. It is far more plausible to suppose, rather, that the courts were designed to be an intermediate body between the people and legislature, in order (among other things) to keep the legislature within their assigned limits. The interpretation of the laws is the proper and particular role of the courts. A constitution is, in fact, a fundamental law. It therefore belongs to them to ascertain its meaning, as well as the meaning of any particular laws proceeding from the legislative body. If there happens to be an irreconcilable conflict between the two, the one with the superior obligation and validity ought to be preferred; in other words, the Constitution ought to be preferred to the statute, the intention of the people to the intention of their delegated representatives.

Nor does this conclusion in any way suppose that the judicial power is superior to the legislative. It only supposes that the power of the people is superior to both; and that if the will of the legislature as expressed in its statutes stands in opposition to the will of the people as expressed in the Constitution, the judges ought to follow the latter rather than the former. They ought to regulate their decisions by the fundamental laws, rather than by those which are not fundamental.

This exercise of judicial discretion in deciding between two contradictory laws is exemplified in a familiar instance. It sometimes happens that there are two statutes existing at one time which clash in whole or part with each other, while neither of them contains any repealing clause or expression. In such a case, it is the task of the courts to determine their meaning and operation. As far as the two statutes can, by any reasonable interpretation, be reconciled to each other, reason and law both dictate that this should be done. If this is impossible, it becomes necessary to uphold one to the exclusion of the other. The rule which has been followed in the courts for determining relative validity in these cases is that the more recent statute should be preferred to the less recent. This is a simple interpretive rule that is not derived from any positive law, but from the nature and reason of the thing. It is a rule that has not been imposed upon the courts by legislation, but adopted by themselves as consonant to truth and appropriate for the direction of their conduct as interpreters of the law. They thought it reasonable that, between the conflicting acts of an *equal* authority, the most recent should be preferred.

But when the conflicting acts are between a superior and a subordinate authority, between an original and derivative power, the nature and reason of the thing indicate the opposite of that rule as proper to be followed. They teach us that the prior act of a superior ought to be preferred to the subsequent act of an inferior and subordinate authority. Therefore, whenever a particular statute contradicts the Constitution, it will be the duty of the courts to adhere to the latter and disregard the former.

Nor is it a convincing counterargument to say that the courts, in judging a statute to be unconstitutional, may substitute their own opinions for the constitutional intentions of the legislature. This might as well happen in the case of two contradictory statutes, and it might as well happen in every judgment upon any single statute. The courts must always declare the meaning of the law, and if they are disposed to exercise WILL instead of JUDGMENT, the consequence would similarly be the substitution of their own opinions for the intentions of the legislative body. The counterargument, if it proves anything, would prove that there ought to be no judiciary distinct from the legislature at all.

If, then, the courts of justice are to be considered as the bulwarks of a limited Constitution against legislative overreach, this provides a strong argument for the permanent tenure of judicial offices. Nothing will contribute as much as this to that independent spirit in the judges which is essential to the performance of so difficult a duty.

This independence of the judges is equally necessary to guard the Constitution and the rights of individuals from the effects of those passions and interests associated with temporary factions. Such factions, which may form among the people themselves due to the effort of ambitious politicians or the influence of particular circumstances and events, have a tendency in the short term to bring about dangerous changes in the government and serious oppressions of minorities. I trust that the friends of the proposed Constitution will never agree with its enemies in questioning the fundamental principle of republican government, which admits the right of the people to alter or abolish the established Constitution whenever they find it inconsistent with their happiness. And yet this principle does not imply that the representatives of the people would be justified in violating the provisions of the Constitution whenever a temporary inclination happens to influence a majority of their constituents. Nor does it imply that the courts would be under a greater obligation to cooperate in such violations when they arise in this way, than if they had arisen entirely from suspicious groups within the representative body.

Until the people have, by some solemn and authoritative act, changed or abolished the established Constitution, it binds them both individually and collectively. No presumption, or even knowledge, of the people's opinions can justify their representatives in a departure from the Constitution before such an act. It is easy to see, though, that it would require extraordinary courage from the judges to do their duty as faithful guardians of the Constitution in cases where legislative violations of it had been brought on by the majority of the people themselves.

But it is not only with respect to violations of the Constitution that judicial independence may be an essential safeguard against the effects of temporary factions in the society. Such factions sometimes extend no farther than to the injury of the private rights of particular classes of citizens by unjust and biased laws. Here also the decisiveness and independence of the judiciary is of vast importance in lessening the severity and limiting the effect of such laws. It not only serves to lessen the immediate impact of those oppressive laws which may have been passed, but it also operates as a check upon the legislative body in passing them. The legislature, seeing that the courts may be expected to raise obstacles to the success of their unjust agendas, are influenced by the very motive of achieving this success to reign in their attempts.

This effect of the courts has more influence upon the character of our governments than most are aware of. The benefits of the integrity and moderation of the judiciary have already been felt in more states than one. Though the courts may have upset some by disappointing their sinister expectations, they have commanded the esteem and applause of all those who are virtuous and unbiased. All considerate men ought to value whatever will tend to bring about or strengthen that role of the courts. No man, after all, can be sure that he will not fall victim tomorrow to the same spirit of injustice by which he may benefit today. And every man must now feel that the inevitable tendency of such a spirit of injustice is to destroy the foundations of public and private trust, and to introduce in its place universal distrust and distress.

That strict and consistent adherence to the rights of the Constitution and of individuals, which we perceive to be indispensable in the courts of justice, cannot be expected from judges who hold their offices for a limited term.[2] Periodical appointments, however regulated or by whomsoever made, would undermine their necessary independence. If the power of making such periodical appointments was given either to the executive or legislature, there would be danger of an improper submissiveness to the branch which possessed it. If it were given to both branches, there would be an unwillingness to risk the disappointment of either. If it were given to the people, or to persons chosen by them for the special purpose, there would be too great a temptation to consider popularity more than the Constitution and the laws.

There is yet another and even more important reason for the permanency of judicial offices which comes from the nature of their required qualifications. It has been frequently and correctly said that a lengthy code of laws is one of the inconveniences necessarily connected with the advantages of a free government. In order to avoid an arbitrary discretion in the courts, it is indispensable that they should be limited by strict rules and precedents which serve to define and point out their duty in every particular case they decide. And it is easy to see from the variety of disputes which grow out of the foolishness and wickedness of mankind, that the number of these cases must unavoidably grow very large, and must demand long and careful study to obtain a competent knowledge of them.

This is why there can be only a few men in the society who will have enough skill in the laws to qualify them as judges. And once we take into account the ordinary depravity of human nature, the number of those who combine this necessary knowledge with the necessary integrity will be even smaller. These considerations make it clear that the government will not have many options of qualified individuals to choose from. And these few qualified individuals would be discouraged from quitting a profitable private practice to accept a judicial appointment if it were only for a temporary term. Such a term, then, would tend to throw the administration of justice into hands less able, and less well qualified, to conduct it with utility and dignity. In the current circumstances of this country, and in those in which it is likely to be for the foreseeable future, the disadvantages along these lines would be greater than they may appear at first sight. It must be admitted, though, that they are far inferior to those which arise from other aspects of the subject.

On the whole, there can be little doubt that the convention acted wisely in copying the example of those constitutions which have established *good behavior* as the tenure of their judicial offices in point of duration. So far from being blamable on this account, their plan would have been inexcusably defective if it had lacked this important feature of good government. The experience of Great Britain gives a shining example of the excellence of this institution.

IV.
Appendices

Key Quotations from the Original
Text of *The Federalist*

Federalist 1

1. "It has been frequently remarked that it seems to have been reserved to the people of this country, by their conduct and example, to decide the important question, whether societies of men are really capable or not of establishing good government from reflection and choice, or whether they are forever destined to depend for their political constitutions on accident and force." (p. 1)

Federalist 10

1. "By a *faction*, I understand a number of citizens, whether amounting to a majority or a minority of the whole, who are united and actuated by some common impulse of passion, or of interest, adverse to the rights of other citizens, or to the permanent and aggregate interests of the community." (p. 4)

2. "Liberty is to faction what air is to fire, an aliment without which it instantly expires. But it could not be less folly to abolish liberty, which is essential to political life, because it nourishes faction, than it would be to wish the annihilation of air, which is essential to animal life, because it imparts to fire its destructive agency." (p. 5)

3. "The diversity in the faculties of men, from which the rights of property originate, is not less an insuperable obstacle to a uniformity of interests. The protection of these faculties is the first object of government." (p. 5)

4. "It is in vain to say that enlightened statesmen will be able to adjust these clashing interests, and render them all subservient to

the public good. Enlightened statesmen will not always be at the helm." (p. 6)

5. "To secure the public good and private rights against the danger of such a faction, and at the same time to preserve the spirit and the form of popular government, is then the great object to which our inquiries are directed. Let me add that it is the great desideratum by which this form of government can be rescued from the opprobrium under which it has so long labored, and be recommended to the esteem and adoption of mankind." (p. 6)

6. "The effect of the first difference is, on the one hand, to refine and enlarge the public views, by passing them through the medium of a chosen body of citizens, whose wisdom may best discern the true interest of their country, and whose patriotism and love of justice will be least likely to sacrifice it to temporary or partial considerations." (p. 7)

7. "Extend the sphere, and you take in a greater variety of parties and interests; you make it less probable that a majority of the whole will have a common motive to invade the rights of other citizens." (p. 8)

8. "The same advantage which a republic has over a democracy, in controlling the effects of faction, is enjoyed by a large over a small republic,—is enjoyed by the Union over the states composing it." (p. 8)

9. "In the extent and proper structure of the Union, therefore, we behold a republican remedy for the diseases most incident to republican government." (p. 9)

Federalist 14

1. "In a democracy, the people meet and exercise the government in person; in a republic, they assemble and administer it by their representatives and agents. A democracy, consequently, will be confined to a small spot. A republic may be extended over a large region." (p. 9)

2. "Is it not the glory of the people of America, that, whilst they have paid a decent regard to the opinions of former times and other

nations, they have not suffered a blind veneration for antiquity, for custom, or for names, to overrule the suggestions of their own good sense, the knowledge of their own situation, and the lessons of their own experience? To this manly spirit, posterity will be indebted for the possession, and the world for the example, of the numerous innovations displayed on the American theater, in favor of private rights and public happiness." (p. 12)

3. "Happily for America, happily, we trust, for the whole human race, they pursued a new and more noble course. They accomplished a revolution which has no parallel in the annals of human society. They reared the fabrics of governments which have no model on the face of the globe." (p. 13)

Federalist 15

1. "The great and radical vice in the construction of the existing Confederation is in the principle of LEGISLATION for STATES or GOVERNMENTS, in their CORPORATE or COLLECTIVE CAPACITIES, and as contradistinguished from the INDIVIDUALS of which they consist." (p. 15)

2. "Why has government been instituted at all? Because the passions of men will not conform to the dictates of reason and justice, without constraint." (p. 17)

Federalist 37

1. "It is a misfortune, inseparable from human affairs, that public measures are rarely investigated with that spirit of moderation which is essential to a just estimate of their real tendency to advance or obstruct the public good; and that this spirit is more apt to be diminished than promoted, by those occasions which require an unusual exercise of it." (p. 19)

2. "Among the difficulties encountered by the convention, a very important one must have lain in combining the requisite stability and energy in government, with the inviolable attention due to liberty and to the republican form." (p. 20)

3. "Would it be wonderful if, under the pressure of all these difficulties, the convention should have been forced into some deviations from that artificial structure and regular symmetry which an abstract view of the subject might lead an ingenious theorist to bestow on a Constitution planned in his closet or in his imagination?" (p. 23)

4. "The history of almost all the great councils and consultations held among mankind for reconciling their discordant opinions, assuaging their mutual jealousies, and adjusting their respective interests, is a history of factions, contentions, and disappointments, and may be classed among the most dark and degraded pictures which display the infirmities and depravities of the human character." (p. 23)

Federalist 39

1. "It is evident that no other form would be reconcilable with the genius of the people of America; with the fundamental principles of the Revolution; or with that honorable determination which animates every votary of freedom, to rest all our political experiments on the capacity of mankind for self-government." (p. 24)

2. "We may define a republic to be, or at least may bestow that name on, a government which derives all its powers directly or indirectly from the great body of the people, and is administered by persons holding their offices during pleasure, for a limited period, or during good behavior." (p. 25)

3. "The proposed Constitution, therefore, is, in strictness, neither a national nor a federal Constitution, but a composition of both." (p. 29)

Federalist 47

1. "No political truth is certainly of greater intrinsic value, or is stamped with the authority of more enlightened patrons of liberty, than that on which the objection is founded. The accumulation of all powers, legislative, executive, and judiciary, in the same hands, whether of one, a few, or many, and whether hereditary,

self-appointed, or elective, may justly be pronounced the very definition of tyranny." (p. 29)

Federalist 49

1. "Frequent appeals would, in a great measure, deprive the government of that veneration which time bestows on every thing, and without which perhaps the wisest and freest governments would not possess the requisite stability." (p. 36)

2. "The *passions*, therefore, not the *reason*, of the public would sit in judgment. But it is the reason, alone, of the public, that ought to control and regulate the government. The passions ought to be controlled and regulated by the government." (p. 38)

Federalist 51

1. "In framing a government which is to be administered by men over men, the great difficulty lies in this: you must first enable the government to control the governed; and in the next place oblige it to control itself." (p. 40)

2. "In the compound republic of America, the power surrendered by the people is first divided between two distinct governments, and then the portion allotted to each subdivided among distinct and separate departments. Hence a double security arises to the rights of the people." (p. 41)

3. "Justice is the end of government. It is the end of civil society. It ever has been and ever will be pursued until it be obtained, or until liberty be lost in the pursuit." (p. 41)

4. "In the extended republic of the United States, and among the great variety of interests, parties, and sects which it embraces, a coalition of a majority of the whole society could seldom take place on any other principles than those of justice and the general good." (p. 42)

Federalist 54

1. "'The federal Constitution, therefore, decides with great propriety on the case of our slaves, when it views them in the mixed

character of persons and of property. This is in fact their true character." (p. 43)

2. "'Let the compromising expedient of the Constitution be mutually adopted, which regards them as inhabitants, but as debased by servitude below the equal level of free inhabitants; which regards the *slave* as divested of two fifths of the *man*.'" (p. 45)

Federalist 57

1. "The aim of every political constitution is, or ought to be, first to obtain for rulers men who possess most wisdom to discern, and most virtue to pursue, the common good of the society; and in the next place, to take the most effectual precautions for keeping them virtuous whilst they continue to hold their public trust." (p. 47)

Federalist 62

1. "The senate, as a second branch of the legislative assembly, distinct from, and dividing the power with, a first, must be in all cases a salutary check on the government. It doubles the security to the people." (p. 53)

2. "A good government implies two things: first, fidelity to the object of government, which is the happiness of the people; secondly, a knowledge of the means by which that object can be best attained." (p. 54)

3. "Law is defined to be a rule of action; but how can that be a rule, which is little known and less fixed?" (p. 55)

4. "No government, any more than an individual, will long be respected without being truly respectable; nor be truly respectable, without possessing a certain portion of order and stability." (p. 56)

Federalist 68

1. "A small number of persons, selected by their fellow-citizens from the general mass, will be most likely to possess the information and discernment requisite to such complicated investigations." (p. 56)

2. "Another and no less important desideratum was, that the Executive should be independent for his continuance in the office on all but the people themselves." (p. 57)

3. "The process of election affords a moral certainty, that the office of President will never fall to the lot of any man who is not in an eminent degree endowed with the requisite qualifications." (p. 58)

Federalist 70

1. "A feeble Executive implies a feeble execution of the government. A feeble execution is but another phrase for a bad execution; and a government ill executed, whatever it may be in theory, must be, in practice, a bad government." (p. 59)

2. "A council to a magistrate, who is himself responsible for what he does, are generally nothing better than a clog upon his good intentions, are often the instruments and accomplices of his bad, and are almost always a cloak to his faults." (p. 65)

Federalist 71

1. "The republican principle demands that the deliberate sense of the community should govern the conduct of those to whom they entrust the management of their affairs; but it does not require an unqualified complaisance to every sudden breeze of passion, or to every transient impulse which the people may receive from the arts of men, who flatter their prejudices to betray their interests." (p. 66)

Federalist 78

1. "The judiciary, from the nature of its functions, will always be the least dangerous to the political rights of the Constitution; because it will be least in a capacity to annoy or injure them." (p. 70)

2. "That inflexible and uniform adherence to the rights of the Constitution, and of individuals, which we perceive to be indispensable in the courts of justice, can certainly not be expected from judges who hold their offices by a temporary commission." (p. 74)

The Declaration of Independence

IN CONGRESS, July 4, 1776.

The unanimous Declaration of the thirteen united States of America,

When in the Course of human events, it becomes necessary for one people to dissolve the political bands which have connected them with another, and to assume among the powers of the earth, the separate and equal station to which the Laws of Nature and of Nature's God entitle them, a decent respect to the opinions of mankind requires that they should declare the causes which impel them to the separation.

We hold these truths to be self-evident, that all men are created equal, that they are endowed by their Creator with certain unalienable Rights, that among these are Life, Liberty and the pursuit of Happiness. —That to secure these rights, Governments are instituted among Men, deriving their just powers from the consent of the governed, —That whenever any Form of Government becomes destructive of these ends, it is the Right of the People to alter or to abolish it, and to institute new Government, laying its foundation on such principles and organizing its powers in such form, as to them shall seem most likely to effect their Safety and Happiness. Prudence, indeed, will dictate that Governments long established should not be changed for light and transient causes; and accordingly all experience hath shewn, that mankind are more disposed to suffer, while evils are sufferable, than to right themselves by abolishing the forms to which they are accustomed. But when a long train of abuses and usurpations, pursuing invariably the same Object evinces a design to reduce them under absolute Despotism, it is their right, it is their duty, to throw off such Government, and to provide new Guards for their future security. —Such has been the patient sufferance of these Colonies; and such is now the necessity which constrains them to alter their former Systems of Government. The history of the present King of Great Britain is a history of repeated injuries and usurpations, all having in direct object the establishment of an absolute Tyranny over these States. To prove this, let Facts be submitted to a candid world.

He has refused his Assent to Laws, the most wholesome and necessary for the public good.

He has forbidden his Governors to pass Laws of immediate and pressing importance, unless suspended in their operation till his Assent should be obtained; and when so suspended, he has utterly neglected to attend to them.

He has refused to pass other Laws for the accommodation of large districts of people, unless those people would relinquish the right of Representation in the Legislature, a right inestimable to them and formidable to tyrants only.

He has called together legislative bodies at places unusual, uncomfortable, and distant from the depository of their public Records, for the sole purpose of fatiguing them into compliance with his measures.

He has dissolved Representative Houses repeatedly, for opposing with manly firmness his invasions on the rights of the people.

He has refused for a long time, after such dissolutions, to cause others to be elected; whereby the Legislative powers, incapable of Annihilation, have returned to the People at large for their exercise; the State remaining in the meantime exposed to all the dangers of invasion from without, and convulsions within.

He has endeavored to prevent the population of these States; for that purpose obstructing the Laws for Naturalization of Foreigners; refusing to pass others to encourage their migrations hither, and raising the conditions of new Appropriations of Lands.

He has obstructed the Administration of Justice, by refusing his Assent to Laws for establishing Judiciary powers.

He has made Judges dependent on his Will alone, for the tenure of their offices, and the amount and payment of their salaries.

He has erected a multitude of New Offices, and sent hither swarms of Officers to harass our people, and eat out their substance.

He has kept among us, in times of peace, Standing Armies without the Consent of our legislatures.

He has affected to render the Military independent of and superior to the Civil power.

He has combined with others to subject us to a jurisdiction foreign to our constitution, and unacknowledged by our laws; giving his Assent to their Acts of pretended Legislation:

For Quartering large bodies of armed troops among us:

For protecting them, by a mock Trial, from punishment for any Murders which they should commit on the Inhabitants of these States:

For cutting off our Trade with all parts of the world:

For imposing Taxes on us without our Consent:

For depriving us in many cases, of the benefits of Trial by Jury:

For transporting us beyond Seas to be tried for pretended offenses:

For abolishing the free System of English Laws in a neighboring Province, establishing therein an Arbitrary government, and enlarging its Boundaries so as to render it at once an example and fit instrument for introducing the same absolute rule into these Colonies:

For taking away our Charters, abolishing our most valuable Laws, and altering fundamentally the Forms of our Governments:

For suspending our own Legislatures, and declaring themselves invested with power to legislate for us in all cases whatsoever.

He has abdicated Government here, by declaring us out of his Protection and waging War against us.

He has plundered our seas, ravaged our Coasts, burnt our towns, and destroyed the lives of our people.

He is at this time transporting large Armies of foreign Mercenaries to compleat the works of death, desolation and tyranny, already begun with circumstances of Cruelty & perfidy scarcely paralleled in the most barbarous ages, and totally unworthy the Head of a civilized nation.

He has constrained our fellow Citizens taken Captive on the high Seas to bear Arms against their Country, to become the executioners of their friends and Brethren, or to fall themselves by their Hands.

He has excited domestic insurrections amongst us, and has endeavored to bring on the inhabitants of our frontiers, the merciless Indian Savages, whose known rule of warfare, is an undistinguished destruction of all ages, sexes and conditions.

In every stage of these Oppressions We have Petitioned for Redress in the most humble terms: Our repeated Petitions have been answered only by repeated injury. A Prince whose character is thus marked by every act which may define a Tyrant, is unfit to be the ruler of a free people.

Nor have We been wanting in attentions to our British brethren. We have warned them from time to time of attempts by their legislature to extend an unwarrantable jurisdiction over us. We have reminded them of the circumstances of our emigration and settlement here. We have appealed to their native justice and magnanimity, and we have conjured them by the ties of our common kindred to disavow these usurpations, which would inevitably interrupt our connections and correspondence. They too have been deaf to the voice of justice and of consanguinity. We must, therefore, acquiesce in the necessity, which denounces our Separation, and hold them, as we hold the rest of mankind, Enemies in War, in Peace Friends.

We, therefore, the Representatives of the united States of America, in General Congress, Assembled, appealing to the Supreme Judge of the world for the rectitude of our intentions, do, in the Name, and by Authority of the good People of these Colonies, solemnly publish and declare, That these United Colonies are, and of Right ought to be Free and Independent States; that they are Absolved from all Allegiance to the British Crown, and that all political connection between them and the State of Great Britain, is and ought to be totally dissolved; and that as Free and Independent States, they have full Power to levy War, conclude Peace, contract Alliances, establish Commerce, and to do all other Acts and Things which Independent States may of right do. And for the support of this Declaration, with a firm reliance on the protection of divine

Providence, we mutually pledge to each other our Lives, our Fortunes and our sacred Honor.

The Articles of Confederation

To all to whom these Presents shall come, we the undersigned Delegates of the States affixed to our Names send greeting.

Articles of Confederation and perpetual Union between the states of New Hampshire, Massachusetts-bay Rhode Island and Providence Plantations, Connecticut, New York, New Jersey, Pennsylvania, Delaware, Maryland, Virginia, North Carolina, South Carolina and Georgia.

I.

The Stile of this Confederacy shall be "The United States of America."

II.

Each state retains its sovereignty, freedom, and independence, and every power, jurisdiction, and right, which is not by this Confederation expressly delegated to the United States, in Congress assembled.

III.

The said States hereby severally enter into a firm league of friendship with each other, for their common defense, the security of their liberties, and their mutual and general welfare, binding themselves to assist each other, against all force offered to, or attacks made upon them, or any of them, on account of religion, sovereignty, trade, or any other pretense whatever.

IV.

The better to secure and perpetuate mutual friendship and intercourse among the people of the different States in this Union, the free inhabitants of each of these States, paupers, vagabonds, and fugitives from justice excepted, shall be entitled to all privileges and immunities of free citizens in the several States; and the people of each State shall free ingress and regress to and from any other State, and shall enjoy therein all the privileges of trade and commerce, subject to the same duties, impositions, and restrictions as the inhabitants thereof respectively, provided that such restrictions shall not extend so far as to prevent the removal of property imported into any State, to any other State, of which the owner is an inhabitant; provided also that no imposition, duties or restriction shall be laid by any State, on the property of the United States, or either of them.

If any person guilty of, or charged with, treason, felony, or other high misdemeanor in any State, shall flee from justice, and be found in any of the United States, he shall, upon demand of the Governor or executive power of the State from which he fled, be delivered up and removed to the State having jurisdiction of his offense.

Full faith and credit shall be given in each of these States to the records, acts, and judicial proceedings of the courts and magistrates of every other State.

V.

For the most convenient management of the general interests of the United States, delegates shall be annually appointed in such manner as the legislatures of each State shall direct, to meet in Congress on the first Monday in November, in every year, with a power reserved to each State to recall its delegates, or any of them, at any time within the year, and to send others in their stead for the remainder of the year.

No State shall be represented in Congress by less than two, nor more than seven members; and no person shall be capable of being a delegate for more than three years in any term of six years; nor shall any person, being a delegate, be capable of holding any office under the United States, for which he, or another for his benefit, receives any salary, fees or emolument of any kind.

Each State shall maintain its own delegates in a meeting of the States, and while they act as members of the committee of the States.

In determining questions in the United States in Congress assembled, each State shall have one vote.

Freedom of speech and debate in Congress shall not be impeached or questioned in any court or place out of Congress, and the members of Congress shall be protected in their persons from arrests or imprisonments, during the time of their going to and from, and attendance on Congress, except for treason, felony, or breach of the peace.

VI.

No State, without the consent of the United States in Congress assembled, shall send any embassy to, or receive any embassy from, or enter into any conference, agreement, alliance or treaty with any King, Prince or State; nor shall any person holding any office of profit or trust under the United States, or any of them, accept any present, emolument, office or title of any kind whatever from any King, Prince or foreign State; nor shall the United States in Congress assembled, or any of them, grant any title of nobility.

No two or more States shall enter into any treaty, confederation or alliance whatever between them, without the consent of the United States in Congress assembled, specifying accurately the purposes for which the same is to be entered into, and how long it shall continue.

No State shall lay any imposts or duties, which may interfere with any stipulations in treaties, entered into by the United States in Congress assembled, with any King, Prince or State, in pursuance of any treaties already proposed by Congress, to the courts of France and Spain.

No vessel of war shall be kept up in time of peace by any State, except such number only, as shall be deemed necessary by the United States in Congress assembled, for the defense of such State, or its trade; nor shall any body of forces be kept up by any State in time of peace, except such number only, as in the judgment of the United States in Congress assembled, shall be deemed requisite to garrison the forts necessary for the defense of such State; but every State shall always keep up a well-regulated and disciplined militia, sufficiently armed and accoutered, and shall provide and constantly have ready for use, in public stores, a due number of filed pieces and tents, and a proper quantity of arms, ammunition and camp equipage.

No State shall engage in any war without the consent of the United States in Congress assembled, unless such State be actually invaded by enemies, or shall have received certain advice of a resolution being formed by some nation of Indians to invade such State, and the danger is so imminent as not to admit of a delay till the United States in Congress assembled can be consulted; nor shall any State grant commissions to any ships or vessels of war, nor letters of marque or reprisal, except it be after a declaration of war by the United States in Congress assembled, and then only against the Kingdom or State and the subjects thereof, against which war has been so declared, and under such regulations as shall be established by the United States in Congress assembled, unless such State be infested by pirates, in which case vessels of war may be fitted out for that occasion, and kept so long as the danger shall continue, or until the United States in Congress assembled shall determine otherwise.

VII.

When land forces are raised by any State for the common defense, all officers of or under the rank of colonel, shall be appointed by the legislature of each State respectively, by whom such forces shall be raised, or in such manner as such State shall direct, and all vacancies shall be filled up by the State which first made the appointment.

VIII.

All charges of war, and all other expenses that shall be incurred for the common defense or general welfare, and allowed by the United States in Congress assembled, shall be defrayed out of a common treasury, which shall be supplied by the several States in proportion to the value of all land within each State, granted or surveyed for any person, as such land and the buildings and improvements thereon shall be estimated according to such mode as the United States in Congress assembled, shall from time to time direct and appoint.

The taxes for paying that proportion shall be laid and levied by the authority and direction of the legislatures of the several States within the time agreed upon by the United States in Congress assembled.

IX.

The United States in Congress assembled, shall have the sole and exclusive right and power of determining on peace and war, except in the cases mentioned in the sixth article—of sending and receiving ambassadors—entering into treaties and alliances, provided that no treaty of commerce shall be made whereby the legislative power of the respective States shall be restrained from imposing such imposts and duties on foreigners, as their own people are subjected to, or from prohibiting the exportation or importation of any species of goods or commodities whatsoever—of establishing rules for deciding in all cases, what captures on land or water shall be legal, and in what manner prizes taken by land or naval forces in the service of the United States shall be divided or appropriated—of granting letters of marque and reprisal in times of peace—appointing courts for the trial of piracies and felonies committed on the high seas and establishing courts for receiving and determining finally appeals in all cases of captures, provided that no member of Congress shall be appointed a judge of any of the said courts.

The United States in Congress assembled shall also be the last resort on appeal in all disputes and differences now subsisting or that hereafter may arise between two or more States concerning boundary, jurisdiction or any other causes whatever; which authority shall always be exercised in the manner following. Whenever the legislative or executive authority or lawful agent of any State in controversy with another shall present a petition to Congress stating the matter in question and praying for a hearing, notice thereof shall be given by order of Congress to the legislative or executive authority of the other State in controversy, and a day assigned for the appearance of the parties by their lawful agents, who shall then be directed to appoint by joint consent, commissioners or judges to constitute a court for hearing and determining the matter in question: but if they cannot agree, Congress shall name three persons out of each of the United States, and from the list of such persons each party shall alternately strike out one, the petitioners beginning, until the number shall be reduced to thirteen; and from that number not less than seven, nor more than nine names as Congress shall direct, shall in the presence of Congress be drawn out by lot, and the persons whose names shall be so drawn or any five of them, shall be commissioners or judges, to hear and finally determine the controversy, so always as a major part of the judges who shall hear the cause shall agree in the determination: and if

either party shall neglect to attend at the day appointed, without showing reasons, which Congress shall judge sufficient, or being present shall
refuse to strike, the Congress shall proceed to nominate three persons out
of each State, and the secretary of Congress shall strike in behalf of such
party absent or refusing; and the judgment and sentence of the court to
be appointed, in the manner before prescribed, shall be final and conclusive; and if any of the parties shall refuse to submit to the authority of
such court, or to appear or defend their claim or cause, the court shall
nevertheless proceed to pronounce sentence, or judgment, which shall
in like manner be final and decisive, the judgment or sentence and other
proceedings being in either case transmitted to Congress, and lodged
among the acts of Congress for the security of the parties concerned:
provided that every commissioner, before he sits in judgment, shall take
an oath to be administered by one of the judges of the supreme or superior court of the State, where the cause shall be tried, 'well and truly to
hear and determine the matter in question, according to the best of his
judgment, without favor, affection or hope of reward': provided also, that
no State shall be deprived of territory for the benefit of the United States.

All controversies concerning the private right of soil claimed under
different grants of two or more States, whose jurisdictions as they may
respect such lands, and the States which passed such grants are adjusted,
the said grants or either of them being at the same time claimed to have
originated antecedent to such settlement of jurisdiction, shall on the
petition of either party to the Congress of the United States, be finally
determined as near as may be in the same manner as is before prescribed
for deciding disputes respecting territorial jurisdiction between different
States.

The United States in Congress assembled shall also have the sole and
exclusive right and power of regulating the alloy and value of coin struck
by their own authority, or by that of the respective States—fixing the
standards of weights and measures throughout the United States—regulating the trade and managing all affairs with the Indians, not members
of any of the States, provided that the legislative right of any State within
its own limits be not infringed or violated—establishing or regulating
post offices from one State to another, throughout all the United States,
and exacting such postage on the papers passing through the same as
may be requisite to defray the expenses of the said office—appointing all
officers of the land forces, in the service of the United States, excepting

regimental officers—appointing all the officers of the naval forces, and commissioning all officers whatever in the service of the United States—making rules for the government and regulation of the said land and naval forces, and directing their operations.

The United States in Congress assembled shall have authority to appoint a committee, to sit in the recess of Congress, to be denominated "A Committee of the States," and to consist of one delegate from each State; and to appoint such other committees and civil officers as may be necessary for managing the general affairs of the United States under their direction—to appoint one of their members to preside, provided that no person be allowed to serve in the office of president more than one year in any term of three years; to ascertain the necessary sums of money to be raised for the service of the United States, and to appropriate and apply the same for defraying the public expenses—to borrow money, or emit bills on the credit of the United States, transmitting every half-year to the respective States an account of the sums of money so borrowed or emitted—to build and equip a navy—to agree upon the number of land forces, and to make requisitions from each State for its quota, in proportion to the number of white inhabitants in such State; which requisition shall be binding, and thereupon the legislature of each State shall appoint the regimental officers, raise the men and cloth, arm and equip them in a solid-like manner, at the expense of the United States; and the officers and men so clothed, armed and equipped shall march to the place appointed, and within the time agreed on by the United States in Congress assembled. But if the United States in Congress assembled shall, on consideration of circumstances judge proper that any State should not raise men, or should raise a smaller number of men than the quota thereof, such extra number shall be raised, officered, clothed, armed and equipped in the same manner as the quota of each State, unless the legislature of such State shall judge that such extra number cannot be safely spread out in the same, in which case they shall raise, officer, cloth, arm and equip as many of such extra number as they judge can be safely spared. And the officers and men so clothed, armed, and equipped, shall march to the place appointed, and within the time agreed on by the United States in Congress assembled.

The United States in Congress assembled shall never engage in a war, nor grant letters of marque or reprisal in time of peace, nor enter into any treaties or alliances, nor coin money, nor regulate the value thereof, nor ascertain the sums and expenses necessary for the defense and welfare of the United States, or any of them, nor emit bills, nor borrow money on the credit of the United States, nor appropriate money, nor agree upon the number of vessels of war, to be built or purchased, or the number of land or sea forces to be raised, nor appoint a commander in chief of the army or navy, unless nine States assent to the same: nor shall a question on any other point, except for adjourning from day to day be determined, unless by the votes of the majority of the United States in Congress assembled.

The Congress of the United States shall have power to adjourn to any time within the year, and to any place within the United States, so that no period of adjournment be for a longer duration than the space of six months, and shall publish the journal of their proceedings monthly, except such parts thereof relating to treaties, alliances or military operations, as in their judgment require secrecy; and the yeas and nays of the delegates of each State on any question shall be entered on the journal, when it is desired by any delegates of a State, or any of them, at his or their request shall be furnished with a transcript of the said journal, except such parts as are above excepted, to lay before the legislatures of the several States.

X.

The Committee of the States, or any nine of them, shall be authorized to execute, in the recess of Congress, such of the powers of Congress as the United States in Congress assembled, by the consent of the nine States, shall from time to time think expedient to vest them with; provided that no power be delegated to the said Committee, for the exercise of which, by the Articles of Confederation, the voice of nine States in the Congress of the United States assembled be requisite.

XI.

Canada acceding to this Confederation, and adjoining in the measures of the United States, shall be admitted into, and entitled to all the advantages of this Union; but no other colony shall be admitted into the same, unless such admission be agreed to by nine States.

XII.

All bills of credit emitted, monies borrowed, and debts contracted by, or under the authority of Congress, before the assembling of the United States, in pursuance of the present Confederation, shall be deemed and considered as a charge against the United States, for payment and satisfaction whereof the said United States, and the public faith are hereby solemnly pledged.

XIII.

Every State shall abide by the determination of the United States in Congress assembled, on all questions which by this Confederation are submitted to them. And the Articles of this Confederation shall be inviolably observed by every State, and the Union shall be perpetual; nor shall any alteration at any time hereafter be made in any of them; unless such alteration be agreed to in a Congress of the United States, and be afterwards confirmed by the legislatures of every State.

And Whereas it hath pleased the Great Governor of the World to incline the hearts of the legislatures we respectively represent in Congress, to approve of, and to authorize us to ratify the said Articles of Confederation and perpetual Union. Know Ye that we the undersigned delegates, by virtue of the power and authority to us given for that purpose, do by these presents, in the name and in behalf of our respective constituents, fully and entirely ratify and confirm each and every of the said Articles of Confederation and perpetual Union, and all and singular the matters and things therein contained: And we do further solemnly plight and engage the faith of our respective constituents, that they shall abide by the determinations of the United States in Congress assembled, on all questions, which by the said Confederation are submitted to them. And that the Articles thereof shall be inviolably observed by the States we respectively represent, and that the Union shall be perpetual.

In Witness whereof we have hereunto set our hands in Congress. Done at Philadelphia in the State of Pennsylvania the ninth day of July in the Year of our Lord One Thousand Seven Hundred and Seventy-Eight, and in the Third Year of the independence of America.

The U.S. Constitution

We the People of the United States, in Order to form a more perfect Union, establish Justice, insure domestic Tranquility, provide for the common defense, promote the general Welfare, and secure the Blessings of Liberty to ourselves and our Posterity, do ordain and establish this Constitution for the United States of America.

Article I

Section 1

All legislative Powers herein granted shall be vested in a Congress of the United States, which shall consist of a Senate and House of Representatives.

Section 2

1: The House of Representatives shall be composed of Members chosen every second Year by the People of the several States, and the Electors in each State shall have the Qualifications requisite for Electors of the most numerous Branch of the State Legislature.

2: No Person shall be a Representative who shall not have attained to the Age of twenty-five Years, and been seven Years a Citizen of the United States, and who shall not, when elected, be an Inhabitant of that State in which he shall be chosen.

3: Representatives and direct Taxes shall be apportioned among the several States which may be included within this Union, according to their respective Numbers, which shall be determined by adding to the whole Number of free Persons, including those bound to Service for a Term of Years, and excluding Indians not taxed, three fifths of all other Persons. The actual Enumeration shall be made within three Years after the first Meeting of the Congress of the United States, and within every subsequent Term of ten Years, in such Manner as they shall by Law direct. The Number of Representatives shall not exceed one for every thirty Thousand, but each State shall have at Least one Representative; and until such enumeration shall be made, the State of New Hampshire shall be entitled to choose three, Massachusetts eight, Rhode Island and Providence Plantations one, Connecticut five, New York six, New Jersey four, Pennsylvania eight, Delaware one, Maryland six, Virginia ten, North Carolina five, South Carolina five, and Georgia three.

4: When vacancies happen in the Representation from any State, the Executive Authority thereof shall issue Writs of Election to fill such Vacancies.

5: The House of Representatives shall choose their Speaker and other Officers; and shall have the sole Power of Impeachment.

Section 3

1: The Senate of the United States shall be composed of two Senators from each State, chosen by the Legislature thereof, for six Years; and each Senator shall have one Vote.

2: Immediately after they shall be assembled in Consequence of the first Election, they shall be divided as equally as may be into three Classes. The Seats of the Senators of the first Class shall be vacated at the Expiration of the second Year, of the second Class at the Expiration of the fourth Year, and of the third Class at the Expiration of the sixth Year, so that one third may be chosen every second Year; and if Vacancies happen by Resignation, or otherwise, during the Recess of the Legislature of any State, the Executive thereof may make temporary Appointments until the next Meeting of the Legislature, which shall then fill such Vacancies.

3: No Person shall be a Senator who shall not have attained to the Age of thirty Years, and been nine Years a Citizen of the United States, and who shall not, when elected, be an Inhabitant of that State for which he shall be chosen.

4: The Vice President of the United States shall be President of the Senate, but shall have no Vote, unless they be equally divided.

5: The Senate shall choose their other Officers, and also a President pro tempore, in the Absence of the Vice President, or when he shall exercise the Office of President of the United States.

6: The Senate shall have the sole Power to try all Impeachments. When sitting for that Purpose, they shall be on Oath or

Affirmation. When the President of the United States is tried, the Chief Justice shall preside: And no Person shall be convicted without the Concurrence of two thirds of the Members present.

7: Judgment in Cases of impeachment shall not extend further than to removal from Office, and disqualification to hold and enjoy any Office of honor, Trust or Profit under the United States: but the Party convicted shall nevertheless be liable and subject to Indictment, Trial, Judgment and Punishment, according to Law.

Section 4

1: The Times, Places and Manner of holding Elections for Senators and Representatives, shall be prescribed in each State by the Legislature thereof; but the Congress may at any time by Law make or alter such Regulations, except as to the Places of choosing Senators.

2: The Congress shall assemble at least once in every Year, and such Meeting shall be on the first Monday in December, unless they shall by Law appoint a different Day.

Section 5

1: Each House shall be the Judge of the Elections, Returns and Qualifications of its own Members, and a Majority of each shall constitute a Quorum to do Business; but a smaller Number may adjourn from day to day, and may be authorized to compel the Attendance of absent Members, in such Manner, and under such Penalties as each House may provide.

2: Each House may determine the Rules of its Proceedings, punish its Members for disorderly Behavior, and, with the Concurrence of two thirds, expel a Member.

3: Each House shall keep a Journal of its Proceedings, and from time to time publish the same, excepting such Parts as may in their Judgment require Secrecy; and the Yeas and Nays of the Members of either House on any question shall, at the Desire of one fifth of those Present, be entered on the Journal.

4: Neither House, during the Session of Congress, shall, without the Consent of the other, adjourn for more than three days, nor to any other Place than that in which the two Houses shall be sitting.

Section 6

1: The Senators and Representatives shall receive a Compensation for their Services, to be ascertained by Law, and paid out of the Treasury of the United States. They shall in all Cases, except Treason, Felony and Breach of the Peace, be privileged from Arrest during their Attendance at the Session of their respective Houses, and in going to and returning from the same; and for any Speech or Debate in either House, they shall not be questioned in any other Place.

2: No Senator or Representative shall, during the Time for which he was elected, be appointed to any civil Office under the Authority of the United States, which shall have been created, or the Emoluments whereof shall have been increased during such time; and no Person holding any Office under the United States, shall be a Member of either House during his Continuance in Office.

Section 7

1: All Bills for raising Revenue shall originate in the House of Representatives; but the Senate may propose or concur with Amendments as on other Bills.

2: Every Bill which shall have passed the House of Representatives and the Senate, shall, before it becomes a Law, be presented to the President of the United States; if he approve he shall sign it, but if not he shall return it, with his Objections to that House in which it shall have originated, who shall enter the Objections at large on their Journal, and proceed to reconsider it. If after such Reconsideration two thirds of that House shall agree to pass the Bill, it shall be sent, together with the Objections, to the other House, by which it shall likewise be reconsidered, and if approved by two thirds of that House, it shall become a Law. But in all such Cases the Votes of both Houses shall be determined by yeas and Nays, and the Names of the Persons voting for and against the Bill shall be entered on the Journal of each House respectively. If any Bill shall not be returned by the President within ten Days (Sundays excepted) after it shall have been presented to him, the Same shall be a Law, in like Manner as if he had signed it, unless the Congress by their Adjournment prevent its Return, in which Case it shall not be a Law.

3: Every Order, Resolution, or Vote to which the Concurrence of the Senate and House of Representatives may be necessary (except on a question of Adjournment) shall be presented to the President of the United States; and before the Same shall take Effect, shall be approved by him, or being disapproved by him, shall be repassed by two thirds of the Senate and House of Representatives, according to the Rules and Limitations prescribed in the Case of a Bill.

Section 8

1: The Congress shall have Power To lay and collect Taxes, Duties, Imposts and Excises, to pay the Debts and provide for the common Defense and general Welfare of the United States; but all Duties, Imposts and Excises shall be uniform throughout the United States;

2: To borrow Money on the credit of the United States;

3: To regulate Commerce with foreign Nations, and among the several States, and with the Indian Tribes;

4: To establish an uniform Rule of Naturalization, and uniform Laws on the subject of Bankruptcies throughout the United States;

5: To coin Money, regulate the Value thereof, and of foreign Coin, and fix the Standard of Weights and Measures;

6: To provide for the Punishment of counterfeiting the Securities and current Coin of the United States;

7: To establish Post Offices and post Roads;

8: To promote the Progress of Science and useful Arts, by securing for limited Times to Authors and Inventors the exclusive Right to their respective Writings and Discoveries;

9: To constitute Tribunals inferior to the supreme Court;

10: To define and punish Piracies and Felonies committed on the high Seas, and Offenses against the Law of Nations;

11: To declare War, grant Letters of Marque and Reprisal, and make Rules concerning Captures on Land and Water;

12: To raise and support Armies, but no Appropriation of Money to that Use shall be for a longer Term than two Years;

13: To provide and maintain a Navy;

14: To make Rules for the Government and Regulation of the land and naval Forces;

15: To provide for calling forth the Militia to execute the Laws of the Union, suppress Insurrections and repel Invasions;

16: To provide for organizing, arming, and disciplining, the Militia, and for governing such Part of them as may be employed in the Service of the United States, reserving to the States respectively, the Appointment of the Officers, and the Authority of training the Militia according to the discipline prescribed by Congress;

17: To exercise exclusive Legislation in all Cases whatsoever, over such District (not exceeding ten Miles square) as may, by Cession of particular States, and the Acceptance of Congress, become the Seat of the Government of the United States, and to exercise like Authority over all Places purchased by the Consent of the Legislature of the State in which the Same shall be, for the Erection of Forts, Magazines, Arsenals, dock-Yards, and other needful Buildings;—And

18: To make all Laws which shall be necessary and proper for carrying into Execution the foregoing Powers, and all other Powers vested by this Constitution in the Government of the United States, or in any Department or Officer thereof.

Section 9

1: The Migration or Importation of such Persons as any of the States now existing shall think proper to admit, shall not be prohibited by the Congress prior to the Year one thousand eight hundred and eight, but a Tax or duty may be imposed on such Importation, not exceeding ten dollars for each Person.

2: The Privilege of the Writ of Habeas Corpus shall not be suspended, unless when in Cases of Rebellion or Invasion the public Safety may require it.

3: No Bill of Attainder or ex post facto Law shall be passed.

4: No Capitation, or other direct, Tax shall be laid, unless in Proportion to the Census or Enumeration herein before directed to be taken.

5: No Tax or Duty shall be laid on Articles exported from any State.

6: No Preference shall be given by any Regulation of Commerce or Revenue to the Ports of one State over those of another: nor shall Vessels bound to, or from, one State, be obliged to enter, clear, or pay Duties in another.

7: No Money shall be drawn from the Treasury, but in Consequence of Appropriations made by Law; and a regular Statement and Account of the Receipts and Expenditures of all public Money shall be published from time to time.

8: No Title of Nobility shall be granted by the United States: And no Person holding any Office of Profit or Trust under them, shall, without the Consent of the Congress, accept of any present, Emolument, Office, or Title, of any kind whatever, from any King, Prince, or foreign State.

Section 10

1: No State shall enter into any Treaty, Alliance, or Confederation; grant Letters of Marque and Reprisal; coin Money; emit Bills of Credit; make any Thing but gold and silver Coin a Tender in Payment of Debts; pass any Bill of Attainder, ex post facto Law, or Law impairing the Obligation of Contracts, or grant any Title of Nobility.

2: No State shall, without the Consent of the Congress, lay any Imposts or Duties on Imports or Exports, except what may be absolutely necessary for executing it's inspection Laws: and the net Produce of all Duties and Imposts, laid by any State on Imports or Exports, shall be for the Use of the Treasury of the United States; and all such Laws shall be subject to the Revision and Control of the Congress.

3: No State shall, without the Consent of Congress, lay any Duty of Tonnage, keep Troops, or Ships of War in time of Peace, enter into any Agreement or Compact with another State, or with a foreign Power, or engage in War, unless actually invaded, or in such imminent Danger as will not admit of delay.

Article II

Section 1

1: The executive Power shall be vested in a President of the United States of America. He shall hold his Office during the Term of four Years, and, together with the Vice President, chosen for the same Term, be elected, as follows:

2: Each State shall appoint, in such Manner as the Legislature thereof may direct, a Number of Electors, equal to the whole Number of Senators and Representatives to which the State may be entitled in the Congress: but no Senator or Representative, or Person holding an Office of Trust or Profit under the United States, shall be appointed an Elector.

3: The Electors shall meet in their respective States, and vote by Ballot for two Persons, of whom one at least shall not be an Inhabitant of the same State with themselves. And they shall make a List of all the Persons voted for, and of the Number of Votes for each; which List they shall sign and certify, and transmit sealed to the Seat of the Government of the United States, directed to the President of the Senate. The President of the Senate shall, in the Presence of the Senate and House of Representatives, open all the Certificates, and the Votes shall then be counted. The Person having the greatest Number of Votes shall be the President, if such Number be a Majority of the whole Number of Electors appointed; and if there be more than one who have such Majority, and have an equal Number of Votes, then the House of Representatives shall immediately choose by Ballot one of them for President; and if no Person have a Majority, then from the five highest on the List the said House shall in like Manner choose the President. But in choosing the President, the Votes shall be taken by States, the Representation from each State having one Vote; a quorum for this Purpose shall consist of a Member or Members from two thirds of the States, and a Majority of all the States shall be necessary to a Choice. In every Case, after the Choice of the President, the Person having the greatest Number of Votes of the Electors shall be the Vice President. But if there should remain two or more who have equal Votes, the Senate shall choose from them by Ballot the Vice President.

4: The Congress may determine the Time of choosing the Electors, and the Day on which they shall give their Votes; which Day shall be the same throughout the United States.

5: No Person except a natural born Citizen, or a Citizen of the United States, at the time of the Adoption of this Constitution, shall be eligible to the Office of President; neither shall any Person be eligible to that Office who shall not have attained to the Age of thirty-five Years, and been fourteen Years a Resident within the United States.

6: In Case of the Removal of the President from Office, or of his Death, Resignation, or Inability to discharge the Powers and Duties of the said Office, the Same shall devolve on the Vice President, and the Congress may by Law provide for the Case of Removal, Death, Resignation or Inability, both of the President and Vice President, declaring what Officer shall then act as President, and such Officer shall act accordingly, until the Disability be removed, or a President shall be elected.

7: The President shall, at stated Times, receive for his Services, a Compensation, which shall neither be increased nor diminished during the Period for which he shall have been elected, and he shall not receive within that Period any other Emolument from the United States, or any of them.

8: Before he enter on the Execution of his Office, he shall take the following Oath or Affirmation:—"I do solemnly swear (or affirm) that I will faithfully execute the Office of President of the United States, and will to the best of my Ability, preserve, protect and defend the Constitution of the United States."

Section 2

1: The President shall be Commander in Chief of the Army and Navy of the United States, and of the Militia of the several States, when called into the actual Service of the United States; he may require the Opinion, in writing, of the principal Officer in each of the executive Departments, upon any Subject relating to the Duties of their respective Offices, and he shall have Power to grant Reprieves and Pardons for Offenses against the United States, except in Cases of Impeachment.

2: He shall have Power, by and with the Advice and Consent of the Senate, to make Treaties, provided two thirds of the Senators present concur; and he shall nominate, and by and with the Advice and Consent of the Senate, shall appoint Ambassadors, other public Ministers and Consuls, Judges of the supreme Court, and all other Officers of the United States, whose Appointments are not herein otherwise provided for, and which shall be established by Law: but the Congress may by Law vest the Appointment of such inferior Officers, as they think proper, in the President alone, in the Courts of Law, or in the Heads of Departments.

3: The President shall have Power to fill up all Vacancies that may happen during the Recess of the Senate, by granting Commissions which shall expire at the End of their next Session.

Section 3

He shall from time to time give to the Congress Information of the State of the Union, and recommend to their Consideration such Measures as he shall judge necessary and expedient; he may, on extraordinary Occasions, convene both Houses, or either of them, and in Case of Disagreement between them, with Respect to the Time of Adjournment, he may adjourn them to such Time as he shall think proper; he shall receive Ambassadors and other public Ministers; he shall take Care that the Laws be faithfully executed, and shall Commission all the Officers of the United States.

Section 4

The President, Vice President and all civil Officers of the United States, shall be removed from Office on Impeachment for, and Conviction of, Treason, Bribery, or other high Crimes and Misdemeanors.

Article III

Section 1

The judicial Power of the United States, shall be vested in one supreme Court, and in such inferior Courts as the Congress may from time to time ordain and establish. The Judges, both of the supreme and inferior Courts, shall hold their Offices during good Behavior, and shall, at stated Times, receive for their Services, a Compensation, which shall not be diminished during their Continuance in Office.

Section 2

1: The judicial Power shall extend to all Cases, in Law and Equity, arising under this Constitution, the Laws of the United States, and Treaties made, or which shall be made, under their Authority;—to all Cases affecting Ambassadors, other public Ministers and Consuls;—to all Cases of admiralty and maritime Jurisdiction;—to Controversies to which the United States shall be a Party;—to Controversies between two or more States;—between a State and Citizens of another State;—between Citizens of different States,—between Citizens of the same State claiming Lands under Grants of different States, and between a State, or the Citizens thereof, and foreign States, Citizens or Subjects.

2: In all Cases affecting Ambassadors, other public Ministers and Consuls, and those in which a State shall be Party, the supreme Court shall have original Jurisdiction. In all the other Cases before mentioned, the supreme Court shall have appellate Jurisdiction, both as to Law and Fact, with such Exceptions, and under such Regulations as the Congress shall make.

3: The Trial of all Crimes, except in Cases of Impeachment, shall be by Jury; and such Trial shall be held in the State where the said Crimes shall have been committed; but when not committed within any State, the Trial shall be at such Place or Places as the Congress may by Law have directed.

Section 3

1: Treason against the United States, shall consist only in levying War against them, or in adhering to their Enemies, giving them Aid and Comfort. No Person shall be convicted of Treason unless on the Testimony of two Witnesses to the same overt Act, or on Confession in open Court.

2: The Congress shall have Power to declare the Punishment of Treason, but no Attainder of Treason shall work Corruption of Blood, or Forfeiture except during the Life of the Person attainted.

Article IV

Section 1

Full Faith and Credit shall be given in each State to the public Acts, Records, and judicial Proceedings of every other State. And the Congress may by general Laws prescribe the Manner in which such Acts, Records and Proceedings shall be proved, and the Effect thereof.

Section 2

1: The Citizens of each State shall be entitled to all Privileges and Immunities of Citizens in the several States.

2: A Person charged in any State with Treason, Felony, or other Crime, who shall flee from Justice, and be found in another State, shall on Demand of the executive Authority of the State from which he fled, be delivered up, to be removed to the State having Jurisdiction of the Crime.

3: No Person held to Service or Labor in one State, under the Laws thereof, escaping into another, shall, in Consequence of any Law or Regulation therein, be discharged from such Service or Labor, but shall be delivered up on Claim of the Party to whom such Service or Labor may be due.

Section 3

1: New States may be admitted by the Congress into this Union; but no new State shall be formed or erected within the Jurisdiction of any other State; nor any State be formed by the Junction of two or more States, or Parts of States, without the Consent of the Legislatures of the States concerned as well as of the Congress.

2: The Congress shall have Power to dispose of and make all needful Rules and Regulations respecting the Territory or other Property belonging to the United States; and nothing in this Constitution shall be so construed as to Prejudice any Claims of the United States, or of any particular State.

Section 4

The United States shall guarantee to every State in this Union a Republican Form of Government, and shall protect each of them against Invasion;

and on Application of the Legislature, or of the Executive (when the Legislature cannot be convened) against domestic Violence.

Article V

The Congress, whenever two thirds of both Houses shall deem it necessary, shall propose Amendments to this Constitution, or, on the Application of the Legislatures of two thirds of the several States, shall call a Convention for proposing Amendments, which, in either Case, shall be valid to all Intents and Purposes, as Part of this Constitution, when ratified by the Legislatures of three fourths of the several States, or by Conventions in three fourths thereof, as the one or the other Mode of Ratification may be proposed by the Congress; Provided that no Amendment which may be made prior to the Year One thousand eight hundred and eight shall in any Manner affect the first and fourth Clauses in the Ninth Section of the first Article; and that no State, without its Consent, shall be deprived of its equal Suffrage in the Senate.

Article VI

1: All Debts contracted and Engagements entered into, before the Adoption of this Constitution, shall be as valid against the United States under this Constitution, as under the Confederation.

2: This Constitution, and the Laws of the United States which shall be made in Pursuance thereof; and all Treaties made, or which shall be made, under the Authority of the United States, shall be the supreme Law of the Land; and the Judges in every State shall be bound thereby, any Thing in the Constitution or Laws of any State to the Contrary notwithstanding.

3: The Senators and Representatives before mentioned, and the Members of the several State Legislatures, and all executive and judicial Officers, both of the United States and of the several States, shall be bound by Oath or Affirmation, to support this Constitution; but no religious Test shall ever be required as a Qualification to any Office or public Trust under the United States.

Article VII

The Ratification of the Conventions of nine States, shall be sufficient for the Establishment of this Constitution between the States so ratifying the Same.

Amendments

Article I

Congress shall make no law respecting an establishment of religion, or prohibiting the free exercise thereof; or abridging the freedom of speech, or of the press; or the right of the people peaceably to assemble, and to petition the Government for a redress of grievances.

Article II

A well-regulated Militia, being necessary to the security of a free State, the right of the people to keep and bear Arms, shall not be infringed.

Article III

No Soldier shall, in time of peace be quartered in any house, without the consent of the Owner, nor in time of war, but in a manner to be prescribed by law.

Article IV

The right of the people to be secure in their persons, houses, papers, and effects, against unreasonable searches and seizures, shall not be violated, and no Warrants shall issue, but upon probable cause, supported by Oath or affirmation, and particularly describing the place to be searched, and the persons or things to be seized.

Article V

No person shall be held to answer for a capital, or otherwise infamous crime, unless on a presentment or indictment of a Grand Jury, except in cases arising in the land or naval forces, or in the Militia, when in actual service in time of War or public danger; nor shall any person be subject for the same offense to be twice put in jeopardy of life or limb; nor shall be compelled in any criminal case to be a witness against himself, nor be deprived of life, liberty, or property, without due process of law; nor shall private property be taken for public use, without just compensation.

Article VI

In all criminal prosecutions, the accused shall enjoy the right to a speedy and public trial, by an impartial jury of the State and district wherein the crime shall have been committed, which district shall have been previously ascertained by law, and to be informed of the nature and cause of the accusation; to be confronted with the witnesses against him; to have compulsory process for obtaining witnesses in his favor, and to have the Assistance of Counsel for his defense.

Article VII

In Suits at common law, where the value in controversy shall exceed twenty dollars, the right of trial by jury shall be preserved, and no fact tried by a jury, shall be otherwise reexamined in any Court of the United States, than according to the rules of the common law.

Article VIII

Excessive bail shall not be required, nor excessive fines imposed, nor cruel and unusual punishments inflicted.

Article IX

The enumeration in the Constitution, of certain rights, shall not be construed to deny or disparage others retained by the people.

Article X

The powers not delegated to the United States by the Constitution, nor prohibited by it to the states, are reserved to the states respectively, or to the people.

Article XI

The Judicial power of the United States shall not be construed to extend to any suit in law or equity, commenced or prosecuted against one of the United States by Citizens of another state, or by Citizens or Subjects of any Foreign state.

Article XII

The Electors shall meet in their respective states, and vote by ballot for President and Vice President, one of whom, at least, shall not be an inhabitant of the same state with themselves; they shall name in their ballots the person voted for as President, and in distinct ballots the person voted for as Vice President, and they shall make distinct lists of all persons voted for as President, and of all persons voted for as Vice President, and of the number of votes for each, which lists they shall sign and certify, and transmit sealed to the seat of the government of the United States, directed to the President of the Senate;—The President of the Senate shall, in the presence of the Senate and House of Representatives, open all the certificates and the votes shall then be counted;—The person having the greatest number of votes for President, shall be the President, if such number be a majority of the whole number of Electors appointed; and if no person have such majority, then from the persons having the highest numbers not exceeding three on the list of those voted for as President, the House of Representatives shall choose immediately, by ballot, the President. But in choosing the President, the votes shall be taken by states, the representation from each state having one vote; a quorum for this purpose shall consist of a member or members from two-thirds of the states, and a majority of all the states shall be necessary to a choice. And if the House of Representatives shall not choose a President whenever the right of choice shall devolve upon them, before the fourth day of March next following, then the Vice President shall act as President, as in the case of the death or other constitutional disability of the President.—The person having the greatest number of votes as Vice President, shall be the Vice President, if such number be a majority of the whole number of Electors appointed, and if no person have a majority, then from the two highest numbers on the list, the Senate shall choose the Vice President; a quorum for the purpose shall consist of two-thirds of the whole number of Senators, and a majority of the whole number shall be necessary to a choice. But no person constitutionally ineligible to the office of President shall be eligible to that of Vice President of the United States.

Article XIII

Neither slavery nor involuntary servitude, except as a punishment for crime whereof the party shall have been duly convicted, shall exist within the United States, or any place subject to their jurisdiction.

Congress shall have power to enforce this article by appropriate legislation.

Article XIV

1: All persons born or naturalized in the United States, and subject to the jurisdiction thereof, are citizens of the United States and of the State wherein they reside. No State shall make or enforce any law which shall abridge the privileges or immunities of citizens of the United States; nor shall any State deprive any person of life, liberty, or property, without due process of law; nor deny to any person within its jurisdiction the equal protection of the laws.

2: Representatives shall be apportioned among the several States according to their respective numbers, counting the whole number of persons in each State, excluding Indians not taxed. But when the right to vote at any election for the choice of electors for President and Vice President of the United States, Representatives in Congress, the Executive and Judicial officers of a State, or the members of the Legislature thereof, is denied to any of the male inhabitants of such State, being twenty-one years of age, and citizens of the United States, or in any way abridged, except for participation in rebellion, or other crime, the basis of representation therein shall be reduced in the proportion which the number of such male citizens shall bear to the whole number of male citizens twenty-one years of age in such State.

3: No person shall be a Senator or Representative in Congress, or elector of President and Vice President, or hold any office, civil or military, under the United States, or under any State, who, having previously taken an oath, as a member of Congress, or as an officer of the United States, or as a member of any State legislature, or as an executive or judicial officer of any State, to support the Constitution of the United States, shall have engaged in insurrection or rebellion against the same, or given aid or comfort to the enemies thereof. But Congress may by a vote of two-thirds of each House, remove such disability.

4: The validity of the public debt of the United States, authorized by law, including debts incurred for payment of pensions and bounties for services in suppressing insurrection or rebellion, shall not be questioned. But neither the United States nor any State shall assume or pay any debt or obligation incurred in aid of insurrection or rebellion against the United States, or any claim for the loss or emancipation of any slave; but all such debts, obligations and claims shall be held illegal and void.

5: The Congress shall have power to enforce, by appropriate legislation, the provisions of this article.

Article XV

The right of citizens of the United States to vote shall not be denied or abridged by the United States or by any State on account of race, color, or previous condition of servitude.

The Congress shall have power to enforce this article by appropriate legislation.

Article XVI

The Congress shall have power to lay and collect taxes on incomes, from whatever source derived, without apportionment among the several States, and without regard to any census or enumeration.

Article XVII

1: The Senate of the United States shall be composed of two Senators from each State, elected by the people thereof, for six years; and each Senator shall have one vote. The electors in each State shall have the qualifications requisite for electors of the most numerous branch of the State legislatures.

2: When vacancies happen in the representation of any State in the Senate, the executive authority of such State shall issue writs of election to fill such vacancies: *Provided*, That the legislature of any State may empower the executive thereof to make temporary appointments until the people fill the vacancies by election as the legislature may direct.

3: This amendment shall not be so construed as to affect the election or term of any Senator chosen before it becomes valid as part of the Constitution.

Article XVIII

1: After one year from the ratification of this article the manufacture, sale, or transportation of intoxicating liquors within, the importation thereof into, or the exportation thereof from the United States and all territory subject to the jurisdiction thereof for beverage purposes is hereby prohibited.

2: The Congress and the several States shall have concurrent power to enforce this article by appropriate legislation.

3: This article shall be inoperative unless it shall have been ratified as an amendment to the Constitution by the legislatures of the several States, as provided in the Constitution, within seven years from the date of the submission hereof to the States by the Congress.

Article XIX

The right of citizens of the United States to vote shall not be denied or abridged by the United States or by any State on account of sex.

Congress shall have power to enforce this article by appropriate legislation.

Article XX

1: The terms of the President and Vice President shall end at noon on the 20th day of January, and the terms of Senators and Representatives at noon on the 3rd day of January, of the years in which such terms would have ended if this article had not been ratified; and the terms of their successors shall then begin.

2: The Congress shall assemble at least once in every year, and such meeting shall begin at noon on the 3rd day of January, unless they shall by law appoint a different day.

3: If, at the time fixed for the beginning of the term of the President, the President elect shall have died, the Vice President elect shall become President. If a President shall not have been chosen before the time fixed for the beginning of his term, or if the President elect shall have failed to qualify, then the Vice President elect shall act as President until a President shall have qualified; and the Congress may by law provide for the case wherein neither a President elect nor a Vice President elect shall have qualified, declaring who shall then act as President, or the manner in which one who is to act shall be selected, and such person shall act accordingly until a President or Vice President shall have qualified.

4: The Congress may by law provide for the case of the death of any of the persons from whom the House of Representatives may choose a President whenever the right of choice shall have devolved upon them, and for the case of the death of any of the persons from whom the Senate may choose a Vice President whenever the right of choice shall have devolved upon them.

5: Sections 1 and 2 shall take effect on the 15th day of October following the ratification of this article.

6: This article shall be inoperative unless it shall have been ratified as an amendment to the Constitution by the legislatures of three-fourths of the several States within seven years from the date of its submission.

Article XXI

1: The eighteenth article of amendment to the Constitution of the United States is hereby repealed.

2: The transportation or importation into any State, Territory, or possession of the United States for delivery or use therein of intoxicating liquors, in violation of the laws thereof, is hereby prohibited.

3: This article shall be inoperative unless it shall have been ratified as an amendment to the Constitution by conventions in the several States, as provided in the Constitution, within seven years from the date of the submission hereof to the States by the Congress.

Article XXII

1: No person shall be elected to the office of the President more than twice, and no person who has held the office of President, or acted as President, for more than two years of a term to which some other person was elected President shall be elected to the office of the President more than once. But this article shall not apply to any person holding the office of President when this article was proposed by the Congress, and shall not prevent any person who may be holding the office of President, or acting as President, during the term within which this article becomes operative from holding the office of President or acting as President during the remainder of such term.

2: This article shall be inoperative unless it shall have been ratified as an amendment to the Constitution by the legislatures of three-fourths of the several states within seven years from the date of its submission to the states by the Congress.

Article XXIII

1: The District constituting the seat of government of the United States shall appoint in such manner as the Congress may direct: A number of electors of President and Vice President equal to the whole number of Senators and Representatives in Congress to which the District would be entitled if it were a state, but in no event more than the least populous state; they shall be in addition to those appointed by the states, but they shall be considered, for the purposes of the election of President and Vice President, to be electors appointed by a state; and they shall meet in the

District and perform such duties as provided by the twelfth article of amendment.

2: The Congress shall have power to enforce this article by appropriate legislation.

Article XXIV

1: The right of citizens of the United States to vote in any primary or other election for President or Vice President, for electors for President or Vice President, or for Senator or Representative in Congress, shall not be denied or abridged by the United States or any state by reason of failure to pay any poll tax or other tax.

2: The Congress shall have power to enforce this article by appropriate legislation.

Article XXV

1: In case of the removal of the President from office or of his death or resignation, the Vice President shall become President.

2: Whenever there is a vacancy in the office of the Vice President, the President shall nominate a Vice President who shall take office upon confirmation by a majority vote of both Houses of Congress.

3: Whenever the President transmits to the President pro tempore of the Senate and the Speaker of the House of Representatives his written declaration that he is unable to discharge the powers and duties of his office, and until he transmits to them a written declaration to the contrary, such powers and duties shall be discharged by the Vice President as Acting President.

4: Whenever the Vice President and a majority of either the principal officers of the executive departments or of such other body as Congress may by law provide, transmit to the President pro tempore of the Senate and the Speaker of the House of Representatives their written declaration that the President is unable to discharge the powers and duties of his office, the Vice President shall immediately assume the powers and duties of the office as Acting President.

Thereafter, when the President transmits to the President pro tempore of the Senate and the Speaker of the House of Representatives his written declaration that no inability exists, he shall resume the powers and duties of his office unless the Vice President and a majority of either the principal officers of the executive department or of such other body as Congress may by law provide, transmit within four days to the President pro tempore of the Senate and the Speaker of the House of Representatives their written declaration that the President is unable to discharge the powers and duties of his office. Thereupon Congress shall decide the issue, assembling within forty-eight hours for that purpose if not in session. If the Congress, within twenty-one days after receipt of the latter written declaration, or, if Congress is not in session, within twenty-one days after Congress is required to assemble, determines by two-thirds vote of both Houses that the President is unable to discharge the powers and duties of his office, the Vice President shall continue to discharge the same as Acting President; otherwise, the President shall resume the powers and duties of his office.

Article XXVI

1: The right of citizens of the United States, who are eighteen years of age or older, to vote, shall not be denied or abridged by the United States or any state on account of age.

2: The Congress shall have the power to enforce this article by appropriate legislation.

Article XXVII

No law varying the compensation for the services of the Senators and Representatives shall take effect until an election of Representatives shall have intervened.

V.

Index

ambition, x, xiii, 1–2, 13, 39, 48, 53, 59, 65
appointment, 25, 32–33, 37, 39, 47, 51, 56–58, 63, 70, 74
Articles of Confederation, see Confederation
bias, x–xi, 6, 57
British Constitution, 30–31, 64, see England
check, 40, 46, 52–53, 62
citizenship, xv, 1, 4, 12, 15–16, 26–29, 43, 45–47, 51, 55–56, 68, 73
common good, see public good
compact, 28
compromise, 22, 45, 52
Confederation, ix, xii, 3, 13, 15, 18, 20, 22, 25–27, 45, 69
Congress, see House of Representatives and Senate
consolidation, 26, 34, 52
Declaration of Independence, xii–xiii
democracy, xiii, 6–10
efficiency, 2, 20–21, 59–60, 62
elections, 8, 21, 25, 27, 37, 40, 45, 47–49, 54, 56–59
England, 24, 63, see British Constitution
equality, xii, 7, 22, 46, 51–52
Europe, 10, 16, see England and British Constitution

executive, 21, 25, 27, 29–34, 37–40, 50, 58–68, 70, 74, see presidency
faction, xiii, 4–9, 17, 41, 59, 64–66
federalism, x, xi, xii, 22, 26–29, 40–42, 52
Hamilton, Alexander, ix–xii
happiness, xiii, 3, 12–13, 15, 17, 19, 49, 54, 66, 73
House of Representatives, xi, 25, 27, 42, 46–48, 50–52, 58
human nature, xii–xiv, 5, 17, 23, 39, 47–48, 62, 65, 74
interests, 1–3, 14, 16–19, 23–24, 36, 38–42, 49, 53, 55, 60, 63–65, 67
common, xiii, 9, 17, 41, 48, 61–62, 66
and factions, 4–9, 72
southern, 46
of states, 52
self-, 5, 40
Jay, John, ix–xi
Jefferson, Thomas, 35
judicial review, 71–72
judiciary, 21, 29–34, 37–39, 67, 69–73
justice, 4–6, 16–17, 31, 41–42, 59–60, 70, 72, 74
king, 31, 63, 64, 68
liberty, xiii, 2–5, 12, 20, 41, 48–49, 55, 59, 64

119

general, 70
public, 51, 68
and separation of powers,
    29–32, 39
and slavery, 43
Madison, James, ix–xiv
mankind, xiv, 1, 6, 13, 16, 62, 74
Montesquieu, 30–31, 35
nationalism, xi–xii, 20, 26–29,
    52, 54
oppression, 2, 8, 41, 69–70
party, x, 2, 23, 62
passions, 1, 2, 4–5, 17, 19, 36–38,
    53, 57, 62, 72
people, American, xi, 1, 12–13, 24,
    26–27, 36, 48, 57
presidency, 25–26, 33, 38, 56–59,
    64, 68, *see* executive
property, xiv, 3, 5, 7, 9, 43–45,
    49–50, 55, 59, 66
public good, 4–8, 10, 19, 24, 42,
    47, 66
ratification, ix–x, 27
reason, 17, 36, 38, 49, 61, 66, 72
religion, 2, 5, 6, 8, 41, 47
representation, 7, 10–11, 22–23,
    42–46, 49–52
republic, xiv, 11, 24–25, 40–41,
    52–53, 64, 69
    and pure democracy, 7–10
    extended, 7–10, 12, 42
    Plato's, 36

Roman, 59–61
responsibility, xii, 17, 47–48,
    60–64, 69
Revolution, xii–xiii, 12–13, 23–24,
    32
rights, 2, 5, 12, 14, 37, 40–41,
    72–74
    of a minority, xii, xiii, 4, 6, 8,
        41, 47
    natural, xiii
    of property, xiv, 7, 45
    political, 7, 44, 49–50, 70
    constitutional, 38–40, 67,
        70–71, 74
    and slavery, 42–45
safety, xiii, 1, 13–14, 60, 64
Senate, 25, 27, 32, 51–54, 58–59
separation of powers, 29–35, 38,
    67
slavery, 42–46
sovereignty, xii, 15, 17–18, 26–28,
    52,
stability, 20, 36, 51, 55–56, 65
Supreme Court, ix, xi, 33, *see*
    judiciary
taxation, 6, 43–44, 46
three-fifths clause, 45
truth, 1–3, 19, 21, 29, 59
Vice President, 58–59
voting rights, *see* rights, political
wisdom, 17, 47, 54–55,
    60, 68